# MOTHER IRELAND

First published in 2010 by
Londubh Books
18 Casimir Avenue, Harold's Cross, Dublin 6w, Ireland
www.londubh.ie
1 3 5 4 2
Origination by Londubh Books; cover by bluett
Printed in Ireland by ColourBooks, Baldoyle Industrial Estate, Dublin 13
ISBN: 978-1-907535-13-0

# Mother Ireland

## Victoria White

LONDUBH BOOKS

*Do m'iníon, Róise Ní Riain*

1

## Acknowledgements

This book grew from years of conversations with a huge community of women since I became a mother. You know who you are. I won't name you because it might imply that you agree with every line I've written and you're all far too feisty to do that.

Thanks also to the people who went on the record in the book and added their voices to this debate. Many others helped me with research in specific areas, including Siobhán Bourke and Sheila Ahern, respectively the producer and researcher of the Saffron Films-RTÉ film, *Whistleblower*; Mary O'Rourke TD, Chair of the Joint Oireachtas Committee on the Constitutional Amendment on Children; and Eithne Fitzgerald, who as a TD published the *Cherishing Our Children* childcare document.

Libraries are the most civilised places in this country and librarians the most civilised people. Thanks to the staff of the National Library and the library of Trinity College, Dublin. Thanks also to Rathmines Public Library and Dundrum Public Library who never turned me away, no matter how many books slid down the back of radiators or were left out on the climbing-frame in the rain.

Thanks to Sandra Dunne for disappearing with the kids on several occasions.

Thanks to my publisher Jo O'Donoghue of Londubh Books, who got his book out of me, against the odds.

And of course, the biggest vote of thanks to the people who sent me on the journey of motherhood: Eamon, who said, 'Go for it,' when he saw me struggling with my desire to write this book; and Jack, Tom, Ino and Róise, who would have preferred if I hadn't written it at all but may one day understand.

# Contents

# 1

## I Enter a Parallel Universe

*Younger women believe they have choices and they are using the freedom to choose. Eventually, men will catch up.*
Catherine Hakim, *Key Issues in Women's Work: Female Diversity and the Polarisation of Women's Employment*

I sometimes wish I could spend the next couple of years sitting with my daughter on my knee. I love the last of the baby in her. I love the stubby little body which is beginning to seem comically small for someone with such big ideas. I love those big ideas and the huge eyes that meet mine without a hint of guile.

My last baby is leaving me. The seven years since she was born have been the best of my life. I knew she would be my last child so I suppose she always had the glamour of the leave-taker. But she also became a bookend for the whole experience of having my four children. From the time I had her, I understood that the grains of sand of their childhood were running quickly through the egg timer.

I had spent most of my life before her trying to force time on. What my last child taught me was that time would force itself on – all I needed to do was savour it. The challenge now was to stay still long enough to watch the buds of my children open. And the lesson in marking time applied to everything else in my life that would also pass: me; my husband; my friends; even life as we know it on this planet.

What was astonishing was that I had spent so much of my life thinking that having a child would be the end of my life, not the beginning. I was saying this the other day to a close friend of the same vineyard and vintage and she told me she'd just met a woman who'd been her best friend at school, until she'd had a baby in her late teens. 'I thought her life was over,' explained my friend. 'But it wasn't. She just had a child – which meant that she now has a beautiful adult daughter. She also has a new partner and a younger child. She wasn't academic and wouldn't have gone on to third-level education anyway.'

My friend, who became a mother for the first time in her late thirties, shook her head in wonder. How could she have written the woman off like that?

But these were the rules by which we were living:

*Don't, for the love of God, get pregnant.*

*If you must get pregnant, sort your career out first.*

*Don't let babies interfere in any way with your career.*

If you were female, middle-class and growing to maturity through the 1980s, the chances are you lived by these rules. And most of us did so quite successfully, so that at thirty-five, I was one of the first among my close women friends to have a child.

It was like crashing through a looking-glass into a parallel universe. Suddenly I had to question why there were rules and why I had lived by them. Feminism, which had guided me to womanhood, gave me no road map for the journey of mother-hood.

It's been ten years since the initial crash and there were two others, one particularly high-impact (twins). Now I live nearly full-time on the other side of the glass: that is to say, I spend most of my time caring for four young children. And my brain has been so rearranged by the shock that I have to say I like it.

What is it I like?

I like the waiting. I like the passivity. Just hanging around, listening, might seem like a fairly embarrassing way to spend much of your time but I don't think it's time wasted because when the kids need me I am ready to help. It doesn't surprise me that 'maternal sensitivity' has been found to be 'a powerful predictor of children's development' in so much research (see pages 79- 80).

My office-bound career, as an editor on the arts desk of *The Irish Times*, was all action. When I think of it I think of the phrase 'Sell, sell, sell!' It was all getting on the phone, banging it down, 'alerting' people to important things ('alerting' was a very popular word in our office). I really hated all that. I did enjoy the parts of the job that were private, quiet and meditative, like editing a long piece of writing or writing a long piece. But these periods were rare.

It was not the work I disliked then: it was the pace and place of the work. I will, however, always feel grateful that I had the privilege of working for such an excellent newspaper. I was hauled over the coals on a daily basis for lapses in accuracy or taste and I often resented this but when I look back I can only wonder at how high those editorial standards were. Now, as a very sensitive consumer of news, I value those standards all the more.

Of course I loved my colleagues but being a woman means I don't need the excuse of a common workplace to keep in touch with people. I loved the excellent pay and conditions. But I so much prefer the work I do now that I have not missed my job for one second.

There's a piece by the late, great cookery writer Theodora Fitzgibbon in an anthology of writing by *Irish Times* women writers, *Changing the Times – Irish Women Journalists, 1969-81*, edited by Elgy Gillespie. Fitzgibbon is all for women's liberation but not if it's going to mean she has to leave her house. In a piece called 'Liberation is a state of mind', she writes: 'Liberation, according to the Oxford dictionary, means "released" and apart from a few isolated occasions, I have certainly been "released" – from the age of sixteen. Personally I'd do anything rather than go out at a regular hour to a job. If I was widowed or otherwise abandoned, I'd infinitely prefer to go to extreme lengths – even to learn Bantu and teach it – to make my home my place of work. For brief periods in my life I have had regular jobs and in retrospect they were the only utterly miserable times of my life.'

At home, you can be mistress of your own domain and that is something which a lot of women value very much. 'Autonomy' is something for which women are very often prepared to trade their financial independence, as the work of Catherine Hakim, economist at the London School of Economics, confirms.

When you are at home you get to build a community of relationships in your local area. You know the shopkeepers, the woman in the library, the other parents at the school gate. You also get to be out of doors and for me this was a major motivating factor. *The Irish Times* office in D'Olier Street, Dublin, in which I worked, has since been put out of its misery but I will never forget the grey room with faraway windows which faced an implacable row of buildings. The highlight of the day was the desperate dash across Westmoreland Street for a sandwich to gobble at your desk.

As well as these practical concerns was a much more fundamental problem: the atomisation of the self. I like remaining whole. I like the person who cooks and eats and brings out the rubbish to be the person who works. In an office, as a cog in a corporate wheel, I felt that my wholeness was masked by my corporate identity. It was as comfortable as wearing a mask all day long.

I would hazard the guess that the atomisation of the self is considered a problem more often by women than it is by men. A 2005 report in the *Harvard Business Review* showed that 56 per cent of high-flying women in American corporate life were bailing out mid-career. Not one of them would return to their old employer. Family responsibilities were not the main reason they gave. It was lack of job satisfaction.

Then there are the kids. After seven years at home with them, I have to be honest and say I would defend this life like a lioness. The grief I would feel handing them over to someone else would be unbearable. Yet it is a grief which mothers all over the world are forced to bear, often, I feel, needlessly, in this still very affluent society. The American psychologist, Daphne de Marneffe, has written a brilliant analysis of society's repression of mother-love,

*Maternal Desire: Our Children, Love and the Inner Life,* which
was – predictably – not mentioned by the Irish media when it was
published in the UK in 2006: 'Many mothers feel torn up inside
being apart from their babies and children many hours a day, yet
they feel realistic or mature when they are able to suppress those
feelings. The terms of the discussion don't admit the possibility
that pleasure is a reliable guide, or that desire tells us anything
about the truth.' If I continue to be honest (and there's no point
in writing this book otherwise) I have to admit that I would fight
even my husband for the role of primary carer. And that's not just
because I think I would rear the kids better; it's because I don't
want to miss out. The clearest example of sexism in our married
lives to date was my response when he offered to stay at home and
let me go on working full-time: 'I don't want to be sitting in *The
Irish Times* while you have picnics in Herbert Park.'

The idea that the role of full-time breadwinner is necessarily
the plummy one in a household is based on the ideology which
says that earning money is what life is all about and that children
are a necessary evil. It is absolute nonsense. While I do know
of couples fighting about who gets to go out to work, I know of
others fighting about who gets to stay at home.

There was much relief in the recognition I felt when I read of
de Marneffe's negotiations with her husband when she decided,
after the birth of her third child, to put her psychotherapy practice
on hold: 'In our marriage, our division of labour worked in part
because we agreed on the nature of "the gift". My husband and I
both felt that caring for the children was a good to be prized;
because of that, we both tacitly agreed that my husband's hard
work was a gift to me. This was the 1990s, after all, and it was no
longer considered an entitlement either for a father to work or for
a mother to stay at home.'

My husband and I came to our agreement in much the same
way and my periodic resentment is exactly like de Marneffe's.
Once, cycling my twin boys home from a remedial appointment
in town, I was caught in torrential rain and bailed out in my
husband's office. He had a tray of coffee and sandwiches on his

desk, with crisps on the side. It preyed on my mind for weeks.

Some days are very hard. Just yesterday, when the millionth jam sandwich of the day was rejected because it had butter on it, I flung it theatrically into the garden. But sometimes it is amazing fun, like when my twin boys boing around the room as 'bangaroos', or when they come down the stairs in their sleeping bags doing something they helpfully describe as 'dangerous rides'. And very often it is quietly happy. Yesterday it was snowing and we all felt the joy of being snuggled up inside together. I ask myself where this joy comes from? Partly it is a return to childhood feelings of comfort. Partly it is the incredible feeling of being able, for this short time, to offer total comfort to another human being. In short, it is the joy of loving and being loved.

Many Irish people hate to hear about people loving being with their children. They'll usually start spitting that it's all right for us because we have x,y, or z. And they're right: we have them all. We have money. We have a nice house and a garden. We are healthy. We have a much-loved dad (We don't see enough of him but we know he's there.) We are very lucky, then, but being lucky enough to have one parent at home, at least part-time, is far from unusual in contemporary Ireland. Why it is portrayed as such is one of the questions I will try to answer in this book.

I have a vivid memory of being half-way inside the oven attending to the dinner when one of my childless friends said to me, 'You're very unusual, being able to stay at home. Close to unique.' I emerged from the oven, spluttering, that CSO statistics for the first quarter of 2010 show that 67.9 per cent of mothers in Ireland are at home full-time or part-time. In 2007 three-quarters of children under twelve in Ireland were cared for at home by a parent. 'Who the hell do you think picks the kids up at the school gate?' I asked my childless friend at the oven door. He hadn't given a thought to who picks up whom at the school gate.

'So what's all this stuff about then?' he asked.

'All this stuff' is about how we want to see ourselves right now. There was a public war around the childcare issue in the run-up to the 2005 budget. An *Irish Times* editorial on 10 October 2005

argued that politicians would rue the day if they did not provide
more childcare:

> For the first time, according to the CSO's quarterly
> national household survey for March-May 2005,
> the number of women in the labour force exceeds
> the number not in the labour force. A majority
> of women are now in the CSO classification of
> employed or available for employment: 51.64
> per cent compared to 35.7 per cent a decade ago.
> Heading into a general election, CSO statistics also
> show that the number of women at work is 776,800
> compared to 539,400 who are involved in what the
> CSO classified as 'home duties'. There are many
> reasons why the changeover in the profile of the
> working family has occurred. The cost of the family
> home is probably the primary cause but there are
> also hundreds, maybe thousands, of high-qualified
> women who want to fulfil their own personal
> ambitions by pursuing a career outside the home.

Of course this change is significant but its implications for
childcare policy are not as obvious as they seem. For a start, to talk
of women, not mothers, is misleading, because there are more
and more childless women and they are free to work like men.
But even to talk of working mothers is misleading, because if you
don't make the distinction between full-time and part-time work
you distort the reality of women's lives. Catherine Hakim has
made a career out of showing how ideology has replaced fact in
reporting women's participation in the workforce. She has shown
that there has been little substantial change in the level of female
employment across Europe for a hundred-and-fifty years, except
for the creation of a part-time work-force.

In 1926, the first census of Saorstát Eireann showed that 32.1
per cent of women were in the workforce. Part-time work wasn't
distinguished as such in those days but there wasn't much of it

about so we can assume that most of these women were working full-time. In the first quarter of 2010 the percentage of women working full-time in Ireland was just 5 per cent higher, at 37 per cent. What changes the statistics is that 21.9 per cent of women in Ireland were working part-time in 2010.

What is interesting about part-time women workers, writes Hakim, is that their primary identity comes from their life in the home. Part-time women workers and full-time women workers have become more polarised in western societies than women and men, she claims: part-timers are far closer in their views to full-time homemakers. 'So where,' she asks, 'does the idea come from that women are challenging the traditional sexual division of labour? From the minority of women working full-time and continuously, it would appear, the group most likely to include media reporters, social scientists and other opinion-leaders who claim to know the trends.'

Which sheds a light on the conundrum of the mammies at the school gate, when the newspapers say they are working.

I have no ideological complex about whether a mother should work full-time or not. Such a complex is, I think, simply absent from the moral compass of my generation. I think a woman should work that one out for herself, according to her circumstances. These circumstances will include how much money she has and whether she has a hands-on partner but also how many children she has, what age they are and how needy they are at that particular moment. These are calculations which no government should ever make on behalf of a family.

What follows is that the 67.9 per cent of mothers working at home or part-time have worked it out for themselves too. I think they know what they're doing and that no government should tell them they don't. As one of these women, I have a problem seeing my life's purpose ignored and denied. I am writing this book to bear witness to the lives of the majority of Irish mothers whose lives are being erased from public record. I want to give them a voice. I want to describe the texture of their lives and the complexity of their choices. I want to do this so that young women and girls to have a fuller picture of their history and heritage and more confidence in making their own choices.

I wish I had been presented with more diverse role models when I was trying to hack my way through to where I am now. Instead, having broken the first cardinal rule, which is – repeat after me:

*'Don't, for the love of God, get pregnant,'*

but having obeyed the second:

*'If you must get pregnant, sort your career out first,'*

I was faced with the third:

*'Don't let babies interfere in any way with your career.'*

Pathetically enough, I obeyed. I remember it hit me when I was up breastfeeding my first baby, Jack, at four in the morning that I would have to wean him to go back to a job I didn't even like. It seemed a bit mad. Being with Jack seemed the most important thing in the world. But like most first-time mothers in Ireland today, I had made my plans even before I got pregnant and I didn't have the brains to change them. We had a mortgage which required my salary. Moving house was a bridge too far.

But more even than the financial issue – which, with freelance work and without the cost of a child minder, might have worked itself out – was the fact that I wouldn't have let it be said I'd given up my job for my child. I would have been happier saying I'd given it up to raise chickens. I didn't like my job but I would have construed giving up my job because of my child as defeat, rather than as positive choice. Just like Margaret Thatcher, who said in an interview that she looked down at her newborn twins and vowed that she would not be 'overcome by this', I was determined to battle on.

'Yes,' nodded my friend, 'You want to give up your job but you don't want the baby to be the occasion for giving up your job.'

My mother put it more bluntly: 'You can't give up your job just for Jackie.'

If not for Jackie, for what? My wonderful, blue-eyed boy is eleven now: a reader, a painter, a footballer and a writer. I am stone, raving mad about Jackie. I can't imagine a better reason to give up a job, a kingdom or a fortune than for Jackie.

That's hindsight, of course. The extent of the joy that is Jackie was not clear to me then. He was four months old and he sure could cry. I advertised in local childcare colleges and found a pleasant young woman from Kerry who gazed lovingly at my baby as if she couldn't wait to get her hands on him. When I pushed my bike off the pavement and pedalled back to work in my new grey suit, I think she was more worried about him than I was.

'Why don't you explain to him that you'll be back when you're going out?' she asked me.

'Oh, for goodness sake, he can't understand English.'

'I tell my dog,' she replied, and I got the point.

Like most new mothers, I suspect, once I was back to work I was delighted with myself because it was so easy. I could go to the toilet when I wanted! I could read the *Guardian* on my lunch-break! Although, it has to be said, I spent my lunch-break in the newspaper doctor's office attached to an electric breast-pump, because I needed to be able to breastfeed at night and on days off. I never mastered bottle-feeding and breastfeeding gave both my son and me a huge amount of reassurance.

In truth I now think it was grotesque to be sitting in an office with an electric pump when my child wasn't even six months old. The 'lactation breaks' which maternity legislation allows you are probably better than nothing but they also demonstrate our failure to give mothers enough leave to feed their babies themselves.

Then, as now, if you're not in a job making PRSI payments you get no maternity benefit at all. Maternity benefit can't be seen as real recognition of the vital and daunting task which a woman has just taken on in having a child. It is a compromise between employers, who need to retain skilled workers, and women, who want longer maternity leave.

Nowadays, paid maternity leave in Ireland lasts for six months, with the option of a further sixteen weeks of unpaid leave. It's still far less than is provided in many European countries; our closest trading partner, Britain, allows a year's maternity leave, with up to thirty-nine weeks paid.

When I had Jack in 1999, Irish maternity leave entitlements were easily the most miserly in Europe. You were allowed only fourteen weeks' maternity leave, paid if you had enough PRSI credits, of which four weeks were to be taken before the birth. You could have found yourself going back to work ten weeks after your child was born. There was the possibility of an additional four weeks of unpaid leave. How desperate the mothers who could not afford to take it must have been.

The company for which I worked generously paid the full eighteen weeks. My employer topped up my payment so that I received my full salary, a multiple of the PRSI allowance of €232.36 (today the maximum rate is €280). Few employers did as much but, as was explained to me curtly at the time, few women earned any more than the PRSI allowance.

I was totally gobsmacked that paid maternity leave could, in practice, fall a full five weeks short of the minimum period of breastfeeding then advised by the Irish health authorities. And what astonished me even more was that I didn't hear a murmur from the voices of feminism (of which, as an *Irish Times* journalist, I was in the thick).

It became very clear to me that maternity leave, which was not introduced in Ireland until the country was obliged to by EU dictat in 1981, was not fully accepted within Irish society. My mother endlessly marvelled at the length of my leave – 'Paid!' she kept repeating, 'Paid!' – while a friend of my own age opined that it was disgraceful of me to reclaim my job after taking five months off.

When Jack was a year old, my growing outrage caused my first breakout from arts journalism into a piece on mothers' and children's rights, which, in fairness to *The Irish Times*, they published on 13 November 2000. I wrote:

> As a woman born in the 1960s and raised on
> 1970s feminism, who started her family late, I

have been horror-struck at how bad things are for Irish mothers and how resolutely silent they are about it. The message is coming through that you needn't be ashamed to present yourself for gainful employment, even if you have a child. This magnanimous stance was summed up in a recent recruitment advertisement for the Bank of Ireland carried in this newspaper. Jackie Dunne was proudly pictured with two youngsters at her knee and a toddler glugging a bottle in her arms. Her responsible job was described as 'not unlike Jackie's busy home life with three children and a long commute; so planning and people management come second nature'. I scanned the advertisement for some clue as to what Jackie was getting out of all of this – a career break, a job-share, a childcare allowance? – but found nothing to persuade me that a week of Jackie's life wouldn't put me in the grave ten years early.

Was a life like this the goal of Irish feminism? Is that as far as it goes? Judging from the silence of Irish feminism, it seems so.'

My next paragraph although couched in impersonal terms, surely described my own experience:

Returning to work after having a baby, the subliminal signals come thick and fast: work harder than you ever did; don't ever complain that maternity cover is too short in Ireland; don't ever mention breastfeeding. The worst thing is, these signals tend to come from women. They seem dominated by fear. And there is another dominating emotion: envy. Older women resent younger women for their paid maternity leave and ability to return to work, because they had to choose between motherhood and a career. Childless women often resent mothers for their 'paid holiday'. The point is, of course, that maternity leave is not a self-development course for mothers. Its importance lies in its impact on the welfare of children.

In truth, I was only beginning to discover what my own role might be in relation to Jack. It takes time to understand new things and time was something of which I had very little. I keenly remember taking a week off when he was about a year and a half old. We got into the bath together. He leaned back and said, 'Snuggy Mummy.' It was very hard to go back to the office the following week.

'Put it down through you,' is a phrase which keeps coming to me when I think of those times. I heard it in a 1996 Galloglass Theatre Company play by Sylvia Cullen called *Broken Ground*, where it is used to tell a young girl what to do with her memories of a child she had in secret and gave up for adoption. There's a lot of 'putting it down through you' going on in a lot of women who now have to leave their babies to go to work.

Secret adoptions are a thing of the past. We can sigh over them in our superior way. But we might do well to think of the emotions that some working mothers are having to stifle.

It was really only when I went on my second maternity leave that I has a full sense of my first child, then two years old. In the several weeks before the birth of my twins, Jack and I took off like illicit lovers whose spouses were about to return. I remember him saying, 'Thank you for the park, Mummy.'

We're scrolling forward, though, because before all that there was a moment of truth in Holles Street. I had already had a miscarriage and thought I was having another. We rushed into hospital. I remember the kind nurses, looking as worried as I was. I remember the doctor whose only comment was, 'You've put on weight,' before he rushed off to take a phone call. From one of his patients at the Blackrock Clinic, he explained on his return. Oh, right. Anyway, there I am with gel on my stomach and the scanner running over it. The baby looks fine, he comments. Then the scanner stops. 'There's another bit of activity there.' My husband and I watch, mesmerised, as a little bubble person floats up the screen.

'What do you mean?'

'There's another child.'

'I have no twins in my family.'

'Well, you do now.'

We could only laugh. And celebrate. Instead of no baby, we had two! A family of three, when we had started so late! We went across to the National Gallery and ate large slices of chocolate cake. I had rung half of Dublin by the time I got home.

It was all very jolly until I began to look like a blue whale; and quite often, because I could barely walk, a blue whale on a bicycle. It was exhausting and uncomfortable. But the prospect of twins did not in any way challenge my sense of my own identity. I did not feel overwhelmed. I felt happy.

It was other people who viewed me differently and because having twins is like an acute case of having a baby, their reactions were instructive. People seemed to think I had turned into a brood mare. I remember working out that while the one-to-one challenge to individualism in having one child was hard enough for them, having two children was seen as effectively cancelling out the woman.

In truth, I colluded to some degree for my own reasons. After having Jack I had decided to stay on two more years as arts editor at *The Irish Times* because I would by then have done a long enough stint to benefit my future career prospects. I had decided all this, with a passion for control typical of women of my age and type, as soon as I got pregnant with Jack, never for a moment considering how healthy he and I would be after the birth. But all had been well and here we were, two years on, pregnant again. My plan all along had been to leave the staff at this point and work as a writer on a services' contract. My employer informally gave me a qualified 'yes' to this request.

Then the babies came. 'Two little men,' as a nurse had

informed me long before. There was a dark night of the soul in
the hospital, lifting them one after the other into my narrow bed
to feed them all through the night until I fell, starving, on my
breakfast. I remember the woman serving out the hard-boiled
eggs: 'God forgive me, they do be like bullets.'

But once I got them home Tom and Ino were the business.
I used to feed them together on a cushion and they would hold
hands, one little dark hand and one little white hand, clasped
together. I remember them giggling at each other so hard that
they would not feed at all. I remember wheeling them around the
streets of Dublin 6, feeling as high as a kite.

Because I had twins, I had a long maternity leave; I had to
leave work a couple of months before the birth as my bump was
then more like a blue whale harpooned and being dragged to
shore. Long maternity leaves can be the enemy of women's career
advancement. You can say that women 'lose their confidence'
while they're off but I think they just get to like being at home.
Which gets the thumbs-down from the feminist establishment
every time: 'I don't think the answer is more maternity leave,'
said Maryann Valiulis, Director of the Centre for Gender and
Women's Studies in TCD, in an interview in *The Irish Times* in
2008. 'It makes it extremely difficult for mothers to come back
into the workforce.'

They just can't 'put it down through them'.

The long maternity leave I had with the twins helped to
consolidate my identity as a mother-writer. I remember coming
around the corner of a house we had rented in west Cork and
suddenly thinking, 'I'm going to be a hippie mummy.' Don't get
me wrong: I am not keen on hippies. But I could understand
myself as a mother in the context of living closer to nature.

The arts background was crucial too. No one who has worked
in the arts can fail to understand that you can do good work for
which you are not paid. I was well able to put my own value on the
work I did. I didn't need to have it validated by the market.

This was all very good luck because if I had been a scientist
or a barrister or a hospital consultant life could have got very

difficult, whether I gave up my job or not. I know a scientist with three children who has stayed in her lab and she is tortured by what she is missing; I know another who left her job and is also tortured by what she is missing.

I was sure I would not have to leave these babies. My request for a services' contract was modest because I was giving up a highly-paid permanent job with an excellent pension. I didn't care at all as long as we had enough money to be going on with.

Then the planes struck the Twin Towers and financial trouble which had been brewing in *The Irish Times* boiled over. The situation was deemed an emergency. Existing contracts were under threat and quite obviously new ones could not be created. I immediately accepted this.

I was terrified of giving up my job because I was the main breadwinner and we had three babies. But I remember wandering around the duck pond in the park in Ranelagh and forming an absolute determination not to go back. It was the contrast of the trees and the light with the dark office that did it for me. I know this is all horribly Wordsworthian but I can only be honest and hope that there are others with whom it strikes a chord.

Then there were the children, of course, and I was by now certain that I wanted to rear them myself. I wanted to open their minds to art and nature. I wanted to teach them values. I know my values aren't necessarily any better than anyone else's one but they are the ones, along with those of my husband, by which I want to rear my children.

Soon after it became known that there was to be a redundancy package I decided to take it although we would not have been able to survive on my husband's wage. It was a leap in the dark, but both my husband and I are like Dickens's Mr Micawber: we always believe that something will turn up.

Four weeks after I gave up my job my husband was elected to the Dáil as a Green Party TD for Dublin South and his pay went up. But what happened beforehand was catastrophic. With the redundancy deal still not on the table and my maternity leave up, I applied for parental leave to tide me over until I could leave. This was refused. I was told I would have to come back to my job for six months to allow the necessary arrangements to be put in place.

Parental leave at the time amounted to fourteen weeks' unpaid leave for every child, to be taken before the child was five; now it's eighteen weeks to be taken before the child is eight. In seven EU countries there are no grounds for the postponement of parental leave. In others, postponement is allowed on serious grounds. In Ireland an employer can postpone leave for six months if the granting of the leave would have 'a substantial adverse effect on the operation of the business'. This clause has been invoked in only one per cent of organisations. Including mine. I do not think there was another EU country in which I could have been forced back to work with eight-month-old twins.

I hadn't thought to wean my babies off the breast as I hadn't thought I would need to leave them. One of them wouldn't take a bottle. Years later I discovered he had a congenital disorder that caused the problem. I will never forgive myself for the distress I caused him by going back to work. For the rest of my life I will cringe when I read comments like this, from Sue Gerhardt's *Why Love Matters: How Affection Shapes a Baby's Brain*: '[This] extended human dependency outside the womb enables an intense social bond between caregiver and child to develop. This generates the biochemicals that facilitate a high level of neural connections and brain growth which will never be as rapid again,' and, 'Early care actually shapes the developing nervous system and determines how stress is interpreted and responded to in the future.'

Because, ultimately, it was I who took the decision to go back. You can say I was forced to, or I would lose my redundancy payment. But I didn't even look for a legal opinion as to whether my absence would have 'a substantial and adverse effect'. There were simply no words I could use in the context of the office to explain how much my babies needed me. Instead, there were the words of calmness and efficiency that I had always used so well. I wanted to be seen to be in control. This was ultimately more important to me than my children's welfare.

In fairness to my employer, I was offered my job on a part-time basis for a period of a year. Then, two weeks before I was due to go back, I received a couriered letter informing me I would have to work different days on alternate weeks. Now, where was I going to find a child minder who would do the same?

I went back full-time and worked through those months: December, January, February, March. I was late for the twins' first birthday party in April, organised by my faithful child minder. I was absolutely miserable and I remember my feeling of revulsion when a dear colleague smiled at me radiantly and said, 'You're doing a brilliant job. It's just as if you never had the twins.'

'Don't resign,' another colleague kept urging. A mother herself, she wanted me to dig in my heels and look for a career break. Another mother-colleague accosted me suddenly outside the lift: 'You're replaceable here. You're not replaceable at home. *You can't revisit this time.*' Urgent whispered conversations that contrasted strongly with our studied unemotional efficiency while on the job.

It was when researching an article for International Women's Day (an extra piece of work, what a fool I was!) that I discovered I could not be held in my job for more than six months after I had applied for parental leave. How typical of a woman like me to know nothing about my own rights until asked to research other people's.

I pretty much upped and left, which wasn't a great way to end a successful career in a happy workplace with colleagues I loved.

However, I now think it is too easy to heap the blame on employers. Employees in Ireland should be given maternity leave of at least a year and a right to part-time work, if practicable, as they are in the UK. But businesses are not social welfare offices and things will never get much better for mothers and children if society as a whole does not begin to value them. There will need to be state mechanisms for doing just that, whether the mothers are in employment or not.

My story is a very happy one because, by chance, my husband's pay went up and he could support us. The story of what might have happened is just as important. What, for instance, if I had been unable to go back to work and had foregone my redundancy payment? What if I had stumbled out into the freelance market with three under three?

The scenarios are essentially the same: the story of how the welfare of mothers and their children is left, in this society, at this time, to the hazards of fortune.

## 2

## A LEECH ON SOCIETY

*...at some point in the mid to late eighties, the burden of proof shifted from the working to the non-working mother.*
Melissa Benn, *Madonna and Child: Towards a New Politics of Motherhood*

I didn't mention the bump under my jumper. If you were rational about it (which many weren't) you couldn't blame me for having two babies at once. But you could blame me for having another baby a year and a half later.

There's no nice way of saying it, really. The twins were ten months old. I was back at work. It was Friday night. On Saturday number four was on the way. Again we could only laugh. That's the sort we are.

Our families were ashen-faced. Our friends were shocked. The joke had gone far enough.

I was delighted. I had always wanted three children, I think because I wanted the adults to be outnumbered. But when I had Tom and Ino it didn't feel like I had three children. Because the twins were the same age there weren't three poles as there would have been with three singletons. The fourth child would provide that.

I have never been so happy as I was that summer. Free at last from my job, enjoying my inquisitive three-year-old and my two little one-year-old men, pregnant with my fourth child and financially stable, I was euphoric. There are wonderful pictures of our holiday in Kerry: me smiling and the twins waddling into the waves, their sodden nappies at their ankles.

The labour didn't go according to plan. My husband later described me as having acted as if I were undergoing execution under Shari'a law. I was on my knees, begging for mercy. The baby bombed out of the back of me. 'It's a girl!' my husband announced and I would like to say that my heart leaped but I was in too much pain for that.

She has made my heart leap every day since. We called her Róise, the Donegal Irish for Rose, after a famous sean-nós singer, 'because her head is like a rose petal,' as Jack said.

After the twins, it was like having half a baby. I hardly remember her crying. What I remember are her sapphire-blue eyes gazing up at me from under her signature pink-and-grey-hat. Quietly supportive. Conspiratorial.

There were crazy moments that winter, the craziest on a dark afternoon when I retired to the top of the dining-room table to feed Róise. A light bulb went on in the mind of one of the twins. Waddling like Laurel and Hardy in miniature, they began dragging a chair towards the table so that they could climb up. I kicked it over, as Róise clamped on and sucked happily, but they righted it and dragged it over again. Finding it wasn't high enough, they dragged a toy box over to put on top of it. It was a scene from Samuel Beckett's *Act without Words*, except that these clowns were always going to succeed eventually.

But I was very relaxed. You get better at mothering with each child you have. Most people stop at one or two children, when they're only getting into their stride. This is good news for the planet, of course; no one with a consciousness of the scarcity of the earth's resources should go and have four children. We can only plead ignorance, carelessness and luck.

I was relaxed, too, because with Róise I was not facing the prospect of having to go back to work. I felt my husband's job would see us through her toddlerhood anyway and for the first time my life stretched before me, my own.

I was terribly excited. I would be able, now, to give the kids my time. They needn't rush through their babyhood. I didn't need to rush them.

But that was only part of the excitement. I also felt free to have an intellectual life. Sitting in an office making newspaper pages to a tight schedule affords little opportunity for intellectual exploration. I was dizzy at the prospect of being able to read anything I liked, write anything I liked.

I didn't realise I was completely out of step with the rules of contemporary Irish society. By these rules being at work equalled an intellectual, progressive, active life; being at home equalled a farewell to all that. Contemporary Irish society had forgotten all about Theodora Fitzgibbon at her chopping board affirming, 'Liberation is a state of mind.' It had forgotten all about everything which had ever been life-affirming for women working in the home.

Caitriona Clear writes in her introduction to her book, *Women of the House: Women's Household Work in Ireland 1922-61*:

> We cannot evaluate women's household work in the past or in the present unless we at least question the assumption that work outside the house is necessarily, and of itself, empowering and liberating for women, and that work inside it is necessarily, and of itself, confining and limiting.

It was only when I came into contact with other people that I realised I was meant to have lost the plot. When I was out at the theatre one night, a former colleague from the arts world greeted me like someone who had returned after several years in a lock-up ward, and said, 'You haven't been out in a long, long time.'

I had been out every day. I had been at the duck pond. I had been at the shop. I had been at the toddler group. I had been at friends' houses. I just hadn't been at the first night of an arts event, which by this woman's reckoning was the only kind of 'out' there was.

I began to notice that I was meeting exactly the same forced, bright greeting – 'You're looking wonderful' – which people who are going through chemotherapy encounter. It means, 'We thought you were dead, but you're alive!' The conversation went no further. I could hardly have an intellectual life, could I? I could hardly be interested in politics, art, religion, gossip, anything? I had turned into a turnip. But I was lucky to be alive at all.

There were a few friends who still believed I had a brain but they did this by completely ignoring the fact that I had four children. I remember a long phone conversation with an old friend in the US which was all about my 'work'. What was I going to do now? How unfortunate that even when they went to school, I would only have half the day to do it in!

I was raising four children. Four tiny people were depending on me, night and day. I was the tomato frame for those four little plants. It was exhausting, fascinating, life-changing. And he never mentioned it once except as an impediment to a full day's 'work'.

It's hardly surprising that women at home with children find it hard to value themselves in western societies: it is official policy to value only women in employment.

As a middle-class Irishwoman born in the 1960s, I have always regarded the EU as my best friend. It was the EU who forced Ireland into providing maternity leave (1981), equal pay (1975) and, having availed of a six-month extension to the deadline, parental leave (1998). Even more importantly, I now see the EU setting firm objectives for the reduction of emissions which cause climate change, in an attempt to give our children some sort of future.

It was a shock to me then to see the EU baldly stating, as part of the Lisbon Strategy (2000) that it wanted 60 per cent of women in paid employment by this year, without regard for what their preference might be. It is more shocking still to see the presidency concluding in Barcelona in 2002, as part of the same strategy, that member states should by this year provide childcare for at least 90 per cent of children between three years old and the mandatory school age and for at least 33 per cent of children under three.

These demands were announced, says Áine Uí Ghiollagáin, Secretary General of the Irish carers' NGO, Cúram, 'without reference to voters in the different countries, or to the parents who actually have responsibility for the children or to the key stakeholders, the children.'

Reading through the strategy, it seems so obvious that it is informed by the values of an older generation: a generation in flight from the so-called 'traditional roles' of their mothers and fathers; a generation that has not yet learned that children cannot be treated as an homogenous group but must be treated as individuals with wildly differing needs. 'Growth' and 'jobs' are to be pursued and the children are to be got out of the way.

We will discuss research into childcare later. But one thing can surely be said without contradiction: different children have different needs. Very few mildly autistic children, for instance, are diagnosed before they are three but the sensory overload caused by an average crèche would be torture for them. And then there are children who are just needy – like my twin boys who were withdrawn from pre-school when found sharpening sticks to kill the teacher.

What the EU is saying, in truth, is that these children don't exist and that their carers, usually their mothers, don't matter. They will not be part of the brave new Europe.

I don't think for a minute that this is intentional. Reading the EU literature on gender equality, it is obvious that its authors genuinely believe that anyone not in paid employment is a problem. The word 'equality' is taken to mean, quite simply, 'having the same job'. To a woman like me who would not like the job her husband does, it reads like an absurdist script.

'Women with small children continue to show employment rates 13.6 percentage points lower than women without children while men with small children show 10 percentage points higher employment rates than men without children,' announce the writers of the EU Commission's *Report on Equality between Women and Men, 2005*. 'This is the result of limited access to childcare and gender stereotyped family patterns.'

The reason that the writers come to this conclusion is, surely, that it is the only one they can imagine. They don't even feel the need to back it up. And the truth is, it can't be backed up. American mothers have higher full-time employment rates than European mothers but less access to affordable childcare. Even when you compare European countries you can't point to availability of childcare as the deciding factor in the work rates of their women: Hakim notes that Germany, France and Britain have very similar mothers' employment rates and vastly different childcare infrastructures.

But facts are not allowed to get in the way of ideology here. What women want is work and childcare facilities are the 'fundamental instrument' – to be wielded like the candlestick in the conservatory – 'for allowing women to enter and remain in the labour market *throughout their lives*' (my italics).

The document appends a series of graphs showing the sorry state of women by comparison with men. These include women's lower employment rates; their higher rates of part-time employment; the gap between women's pay and men's; their far lower numbers as members of parliament, managers, as executives in the top fifty publicly quoted companies and as full professors in universities. These are all areas of interest. But although the report is meant to be concerned with 'equality', not just 'earning capacity', it appends no graphs showing how relatively poor is men's access to their children, to friends and to their communities and how relatively short are their lives.

Diversity of opinion as to what 'equality' means does not seem to be allowed at EU level. Representing carers at home through the campaign group Cúram, which is affiliated to the European NGO *Fédération Européenne des Femmes Actives au Foyer* (European Federation of Unpaid Parents and Carers at Home), Áine Uí Ghiollagáin says that she was at first shouted down before she had a chance to say anything. Then chance intervened. She had been making bread and had taken off her wedding ring. Suddenly, she got a hearing. 'People didn't want to be seen shouting down someone who could be a single mother.' She left the rings off for a year in order to make some progress.

As a single mother, she was worth listening to. As a married women caring for a child, she was considered, she says, 'a leech on society.'

'We are treated like we want women to be kept at home,' she explains. 'Which is not the point.' What they are about, she says, is respect and rights for home-carers: 'Recognising and supporting all women's work equally with the idea that there could be more than one path to economic independence.'

But this is not a voice that is allowed to be heard because, says Uí Ghiollagáin, it is 'against the culture of an orthodoxy' to allow such diversity of opinion. The traditional feminists on the European Women's Lobby have gained access to power after a long fight and perhaps, says Uí Ghiollagáin, they're treating her as they were treated themselves. Her problem is that her ideas are new. 'I'm part of the women's movement. At the start these ideas won't be taken up. But I'll bang away at them anyway.'

The EU, she says, sees people only as producers or consumers, not humans, and she adds: 'It's better not to build a super-state until you have a human rights framework.' To that end she is working towards the EU adopting the UN Beijing Platform for Action (1995) which makes several recommendations that women's unpaid work should be counted and reflected in the auditing of the economy. If this happened, says Uí Ghiollagáin, her argument would be made for her.

When you meet Áine Uí Ghiollagáin, a tall, bespectacled woman of forty-two, American but married to an Irish academic and living in Connemara, it becomes immediately clear that she has not stayed at home to rear her one daughter because she was too stupid to do anything else. A former teacher with a master's degree in applied linguistics, she speaks Irish like a native, as well as Polish, French, Swedish, German and Spanish – and she's learning Slovak.

She never expected she'd be a stay-at-home parent but when her daughter was born in 1999, she says, 'everything changed'. She quickly realised that she did not want to leave her and go back to her teaching job, especially as she would have to get into the car at five in the morning and commute from Meath to Dublin. The decision was hugely positive for her. She could not get over the excitement of, as she puts it, 'seeing life through her eyes'.

'Your child will listen to you much more closely than your students would. All the things I would have learned about teaching came to the fore. I would have done a lot of work in language and cognitive development. To do it – not on a paid basis – was fantastic.'

But there was more to it than that; she became an activist campaigning for carers' rights. 'That's what happens. As soon as parents at home have a minute they do something else. It provides them with a way of expanding their skills and very often they contribute to the community.'

Áine Uí Ghiollagáin's mother-in-law was Nora Gilligan, who founded the campaign for carers' rights and precursor to Cúram, Women in the Home (WITH), after a meeting in the Mansion House in 1981. Uí Ghiollagáin at first had 'no interest' in Gilligan's campaign but she used her linguistic skills to help out with communicating with FEFAF. She also rowed in to help with the care of her Down's Syndrome sister-in-law. But she didn't connect personally with the campaign until she was sitting in her car during the winter of 2000 and heard the then Minister for Finance, Charlie McCreevy, talking to Eamonn Dunphy on Newstalk. Efforts to track down this interview have failed. But Uí Ghiollagáin remembers him defending his decision to bring in tax individualisation, which removed the tax free allowance for a stay-at-home spouse on the earner's income, by asking why he should pay for women to sit around drinking coffee.

'I could see immediately that this would provide a challenge to anyone who wanted to stay at home – man or woman. And it made no distinction between those described as "sitting on their hands" and those caring for a disabled child, for instance.' Uí Ghiollagáin could also see the difficulties it would pose for people on low incomes. Her decision to become an activist was taken like this: 'I knew that I personally would be all right. But as I had a daughter I wanted to be sure she would be too.'

Needless to say, tax individualisation is promoted at EU level, because it propels women into the workplace. Individualisation was also well supported in many sections of the Irish media, including *The Irish Times*; an editorial on 10 October 2005 claiming that a majority of women were in employment, said: 'Former Minister of Finance, Charlie McCreevy was ahead of his time when he set out his individualisation policy to deal with changing demographic trends in 1999.' (see page 90).

There is, of course, a very strong case for freeing the payment to the carer in the home from the earning spouse's income. For a start, the spouse's tax allowance was paid only to people in the tax system and only to married people at that. And why should the work of care be recognised only as a kickback from an earning partner's salary?

The Commission on the Family made these points in *Strengthening Families for Life,* their final report to the Minister for Social, Community and Family Affairs, in 1998. They speak of the 'so far, unacknowledged hidden costs in rearing children': income foregone if a parent is at home and childcare costs if both parents work outside the home. They say that there was a consensus in the submissions that crèches/nurseries, pre-school and after-school services were urgently required and not just for parents who work outside the home. They were not promoted as a substitute for home-rearing, which was supported as a way of life in a huge number of submissions:

> Over 20 per cent of all submissions to the Com-
> mission raised issues to do with the recognition
> of women's unwaged work in the home. In almost
> all these submissions it was suggested that there
> should be some form of direct payment to mothers
> working full-time at home. Various suggestions
> were made for a weekly allowance, increased child
> benefit, pension entitlements and tax credits for the
> unwaged worker in his or her own right.
>
> Many submissions expressed concern about
> women in low-paid employment who were only

marginally better off working after their childcare
and going to work expenses were taken into account.
Most submissions on this issue took the view that
many women, if given the choice, would prefer
to take time out of the workforce to be at home
with their children. The dominant view was that
these parents should be assisted in that choice. In
addition to the pressures on parents balancing work
and family life, submissions looked for support
for mothers in their important job and for rights
to further education and opportunities to take on
training.

The Commission suggested several models of payment to
parents of children in their early years: a 'parent allowance' to
the parent working in the home; a flexible 'childcare allowance';
extended paid parental leave; and a special rate of child benefit for
children under three.

Charlie McCreevy took on board the recommendation on tax
individualisation. The problem was, he forgot the direct payment.
This acts against the recommendations of the Commission on the
Family in that it propels parents out of the home. It could result in
a loss of income as high as €7584 a year for a couple in which only
one partner works.

The home carers' credit amounts to €900 a year, which Áine
Ui Ghiollagáin describes as 'pathetic'. Cúram wants, instead, a
taxable 'care and education' credit for every child in the state.
The carer would also get recognition, as this taxed income would
afford him or her social welfare and pension rights. Áine Uí
Ghiollagáin says the lobby that wants women in the workplace
to promote growth never do all the sums. They never count the
value of voluntary work, the care, not just of children, but of other
dependents. She says it costs at least eight times as much to keep
an elderly person in a nursing home than at home with a carer on
carer's allowance and that's without including capital costs.

She laughs a lot but at times anger is bubbling under the

surface. She admits she tells people she's a housewife just to 'get up people's noses': 'Part of the difficulty is that we don't have a word for what we do. If we say "housewife" it's the 1930s and if we say "'homemaker" it's the 1950s. So we say, "Oh, I'm on a break from work." Or, "I'm taking an unpaid extension to my maternity leave." The idea that you don't have a word for the profession – if we don't have a word to describe what we do it must be very, very low on the value scale. If all the words we use to describe it are unacceptable – what does that say?'

There are strong arguments within traditional capitalism, focused on short-term growth, for forcing women out of the home. Many of the people who regard women in the home as second-class citizens would not accept those arguments but they have acted on them subliminally by creating a hierarchy of values. The traditional undervaluing of both women and children was far from over – particularly in Ireland – before the most recent and most aggressive phase of capitalism began to look for more workers.

This is surely why I have heard the extreme capitalist vision of volume two of the OECD's *Babies and Bosses* series, *Reconciling Work and Family Life: Ireland, Austria and Japan* (2003), being taken seriously as valid social policy in Ireland.

The OECD, an organisation of thirty countries committed to the market economy and democracy, is concerned with growing the economies of member countries. By 'growth' they do not mean spiritual growth, you understand: they mean growth in GDP. Steering by these lights, they see a parent at home as a waste of time. On this subject this well-written, well-researched and very useful document does not mince its words:

> Potentially the gender equitable society holds the key to substantial labour market gains as it fosters a more efficient use to available labour market resources. However, these gains are not fully realised as many mothers do not find the time to be in regular employment. They are often

> forced to either take up low-status part-time work
> – as this is the only way they can reconcile work
> and care responsibilities – or withdraw from the
> labour market for a considerable length of time,
> if not indefinitely. As a result, human capital (and
> investment therein) goes to waste.

A couple of pages later the document includes the finding that only one per cent of Irish part-time workers reported wanting to work more hours; so the idea of women being forced into part-time employment is the authors' own. Instead, they would like to force women in the other direction, into what they call 'regular employment.' Thus they applaud the Irish tax system, for being 'essentially neutral' in how it treats second wage-earners and spouses in the home.

How can you call a gap of up to €7584 a 'neutral' tax policy? I suppose if you regard what the report calls 'minding children' as not being work, then it is a neutral policy not to reward it at all. I mean, why even give these women child benefit? This is how the authors make the case for axing child benefit for stay-at-home parents:

> While raising cash transfers to families gives parents
> more choice, as it improves their financial situation,
> it also makes it financially more attractive for
> second earners in couple families to stay at home.
> To counteract that effect, as well as enhancing
> objectives to increase female labour supply and
> gender equity, one option would be to link childcare
> benefit payments and/or future increases in these
> payments to using childcare support, at least in part.

I had to read this several times before I believed what I saw. But this shocking and possibly unconstitutional suggestion met no opposition at all.

But hold on, there's another good that mothers produce. Not

just semi-conductors and widgets but babies! What happens if they stop producing babies! Consternation in the OECD. How can we keep these women producing the widgets and the babies at the same time? With difficulty, is the answer, so the OECD has come up with the idea of replacing the babies not born with women in the workplace. *Babies and Bosses* includes a chart (2.5) to show how it could be done:

> The effect (of falling birthrates) could be, at least partly, offset by increasing employment amongst women and mothers. Increasing labour force participation rates to the same level as those of men could have a huge effect on the size of the labour force, especially in Japan. Both in Austria and Japan, the labour force would then be of a similar size as it is today.

This shows how far their avowed concern for men's culture of long hours really goes: they want the women to have just as much fun as the men.

# 3

## ARE YOU FOR US OR AGAINST US?
## TRADITIONAL IRISH FEMINISM AND MOTHERHOOD

*...carrying, delivering and nurturing a baby is an integral part of most women's self-fulfilment and cannot be of men's. That is the crux of the gender difference. As long as it is assumed that society will continue to be organised by men, according to a distinctively male model to which every individual aspires, it will remain too dangerous a differentiation for women to acknowledge. But is that not the assumption itself that needs rethinking?*

Penelope Leach, *Children First*

Sitting in the van reading *The Irish Times*. Hear her mumbling away behind me but I'm paying no attention. It's something about her tummy. 'I don't want it in the tummy.' Then I hear, 'And the other reason I don't want children is that then I wouldn't be able to do my job.'

She's got my attention now. *The Irish Times* is on the passenger seat. It's a fork on the road! She'll decide she won't have children and I'll have no grandchildren! Or else she'll give up on all her ambitions!

'*Of course* you can have a job and children.'

The internal lie detector is going mad. Number three comes out of his art class and we drive off. But when I'm lying beside her in her bed after story time, she starts again,

'If I have children I can't do the job I want.'

'I'll look after your children.'

I could be eighty. Oh well.

'But then they won't see their mummy.'

Point taken.

'I don't want a job like Daddy's, going out every day,' she goes on. 'I want to be an artist or a writer or a cook.'

'Well then you can do it at home, as well as have children.'

'How can I do my work?'

How indeed?

'You can work when they're at school.'

She is not satisfied.

She is six.

My alarm that she might give up on motherhood is even greater than my alarm that she might give up on career. I suppose that's because I am projecting on to her my own horror that I nearly missed out on children. That is probably a reversal of the position of mothers of the previous generation, second-wave feminists, who either missed out on career or nearly did. I want her to have the option of both.

My instinct to reassure her that children and careers are easily combined is troublingly dishonest. I suppose it's that I don't want her to narrow her options *now*. She may never have children. She may come up with a cure for cancer. She may come up with some revolutionary way to combine motherhood with career. (I didn't mention, did I, that she's the most beautiful, brilliant, wonderful little girl in the world? Well, it's a fact. I should know, I'm her mother.)

A few days later, I realise I'm not deceiving her as badly as I had thought. What I haven't explained is that life can have different seasons. The Americans have come up with the term 'sequencing' to describe the concept that we can have different lives, one after the other. This is how the vast majority of women live in the developed world. They work full-time, they have children, they work part-time.

People live long, healthy lives now, particularly women. I was able to get a whole career in journalism out of the way before I had children.

So should I just launch her off into a career and watch her go splat on the wall of her biology as my generation did? Should I pretend that stopping and starting and going part-time have no cost?

There are many, many jobs that would never be offered on a part-time basis and some which could not be. They are all jobs with either prestige or responsibility or both. You can't be at the cutting edge of science research if you're not cutting all the time; you can't be a top-level medic if you're not seeing enough patients; you can't be a part-time national politician; you can't be a part-time priest (but then you can't be a woman priest if you're a Catholic, so most of you can relax on that score).

When I was offered my own editor's job in *The Irish Times* on a temporary part-time basis, I made the point to my employer that I did not think it was a job that could be split. The work could not be cleanly divided between days, so that hours would have to be spent briefing and debriefing, for a start. Then, an editor's style is quite personal and there would either be fights as to the editorial direction or a situation where one person ordered and another served. A part-time editor's job would be possible on a page that was not published full-time; or you could work as a sub-editor, essentially interpreting the decisions of a full-time editor above you. And you might not fancy that.

So the reality is that there are stark choices to be made.

Research published by the ESRI in 2000 (Tim Callan (ed.), *How Unequal? Men and Women in the Irish Labour Market*) did not find a significant gap in hourly wages between full-time and part-time workers. What they did find was a large gap in wages between men and women because women typically spend less time in the workplace. They take time off because they have children. This means they have less work experience and less time to climb ladders.

A table shows men in the workplace, having, typically, eighteen years' experience, while women have twelve. Women tend to be absent from the workforce for nearly five years; men, typically, for less than a year. The book summarises:

On average, women's hourly wages are now about
85 per cent of the average male wage. About three-
quarters of the gap between men's and women's
hourly wages can be attributed to the fact that
women, under current social and economic
structures, typically spend less time in the labour
market than men and more time as carers in the
home. Unless men and women were to become
much more similar in this respect – and views will
differ as to whether or not this should happen –
then complete equality of labour market outcome is
not the appropriate yardstick for a policy aiming at
equality of opportunity.

I would prefer that men become more like women in their
relationship with the labour market than for us to become more
like them. But women's relative poverty and lack of influence are
still important issues.

It seems to me that the only way back for women is for society
to re-evaluate parenting, both financially and morally, so that the
time spent parenting is not seen as time lost. Fine Gael Senator
Frances Fitzgerald, a member of the Second Commission on
the Status of Women (1993), who had three small children in
her early feminist days, came to politics and activism initially
through Cuidiú, the Irish Childbirth Trust. She has a long record
of public commitment to the idea of parenting and specifically
motherhood as valuable job experience. She made the point
eloquently as early as 1993 at the McGill Summer School.
Speaking of the difficulty of implementing the recommendations
of the Second Commission on the Status of Women on quotas
and female representation on state boards, she made these
memorable comments:

We've spent the last half century being told that
women are doing *the* most important, the most
crucial, the most difficult job of all: home-making

and child-rearing, but when it comes to selecting someone to sit on an enterprise board, a woman who has done this important, crucial, difficult, valued job is kind of unqualified. Well, doesn't that speak volumes about the emptiness of the verbiage used to pat us on the head down through the years?

It reminds me forcibly of the time a few years ago when I was asked to go on the political radio show, *Vincent Browne Tonight*, to talk about childcare. Presumably I had been asked because I had done some work on this issue for Browne's current affairs magazine *Village*. But when I arrived at the studios, the producer or researcher asked who I was: did I represent a woman's group?

I stubbornly insisted that my qualification to speak was the fact that I was rearing four children at home. But Browne eased the general consternation by coming in and announcing that I was a journalist.

It's bad enough being disqualified from sitting on a state board because of time out of the workplace rearing children but to be disqualified from speaking about children because one is rearing children is richer still.

When I spoke to her recently, Frances Fitzgerald made a strong plea for putting a monetary value on parenting. She was Chairwoman of the National Women's Council of Ireland and its representative on the Second Commission on the Status of Women and she says the NWCI considered the question of how to value the unpaid work of women in the home. They often thought it should appear in the budget as part of GNP: 'Once you put a value on something you realise what you do. That applies to the psychological, the social and everything else.'

Then why, as a member of the Second Commission on the Status of Women, did she sign the report which explained why it recommended against a state payment to women in the home with this sentence: 'In essence, the maintenance of a full-time homemaker, although of benefit to society, is primarily a private benefit to the earning partner, and as such could hardly be deemed to warrant a state payment.' This is the most patriarchal interpretation possible of a woman's work in the home. It seems to envisage a woman shining her husband's cufflinks and ironing his shirts, rather than rearing the next generation.

Fitzgerald takes the report in her hands and reads and rereads the sentence. She seems bemused. In the end, she says, 'Well, it's of its time.'

She continues, 'If you'd asked me twenty years ago what I would like women to have I would not have said commuting from the midlands and not seeing their children for eight or nine hours. It's not very good for women's mental health, or for families' mental health, or for children's, I would say.' She adds, 'Ironically, women often have less choice now.'

Undoubtedly the scope of women's choice has been narrowed by the financial penalty placed on women in the home by tax individualisation, which has been endorsed by all the official organs of Irish feminism. Fitzgerald says she wanted a raft of other social policies to be brought in with it, that it shouldn't have been brought in on its own.

Fellow Commission-member, Judge Catherine McGuinness, describes individualisation as 'very discouraging to women who want to stay at home – I do think another look could be taken at it. It discriminates against parents in the home.'

She describes the sentence in the Commission's report which described a payment to a parent in the home as 'primarily a private benefit to the earning partner', as 'old-fashioned in today's terms because it was concentrating too much on economic independence and independence within the family as a sort of reaction against the patriarchy.'

The trade union voice was very strong, she explains, as was that of the employers' representatives, and they represented employed people. She describes the recommendation against a payment to the parent in the home as, 'not very logical – if you campaign for someone to look after your children, why not yourself?'

The truth is that we have been no different in Ireland from the rest of the developed world, in having a feminist ideology which has failed to recognise fully the importance of care work.

I was well advanced in my critique of the report of the Second Commission on the Status of Women before I remembered that I had owned a copy. It had done long service as a lamp stand in my first home. Why had I had it, I wondered?

Eventually I remembered that I had reported on it in *The Irish Times* when it came out. And I had recorded the now offending statement about a state payment to women in the home with barely-disguised glee.

It was some put-down. Particularly when you consider that the Second Commission on the Status of Women, established by Taoiseach Charles Haughey in 1990 under the chairmanship of Judge Mella Carroll, was asked to pay special attention to the needs of women in the home. And of the six hundred and three submissions received by the Commission, the item sought by the largest number of submissions was some payment for women in the home.

The Commission made some excellent recommendations. My favourite is 'community of property', which would give both partners in marriage (and, today, in civil partnership) joint ownership of all the household's income: 'In all justice,' says the report, 'the wife working in the home is entitled to a share in the family income, as of right, instead of just being maintained.'

I couldn't agree more. But the three progress reports on the implementation of the Second Commission have said no more about this but that bringing in 'community of property' would need constitutional change.

The position of the woman in the home is considered here as an equality issue between men and women, rather than an issue of wider social concern – or of concern to children. It is almost as if the Second Commission feared that any recognition of the social worth of parenting would force women to parent. In the report of the First Commission on the Status of Women (1971), chaired by Thekla Beere, there seems to be no such fear. Something happened between 1971 and 1993 that turned Irish

feminism from supporting women in their caring role to trying
to get them out of it. Surely it was the dawning, in the 1980s, of
the era of exponential economic growth worldwide, following the
deregulation of the Thatcher and Reagan administrations. This
was the era in which was born the type of feminist which Melissa
Benn calls 'bourgeois feminist triumphalist'.

The difference in tone and ideology between the reports of
the First and the Second Commission is stark. There is a lovely
paragraph in the Report of the First Commission that states:

> It is sometimes argued that investment in the
> education of girls is, in comparison with the
> education of boys, largely a wasted investment
> because girls normally provide a return on the in-
> vestment only for a relatively few years between
> leaving school and getting married and that the
> older the age to which the girl remains in full-time
> education the less the return on the investment. We
> cannot accept that this argument has any validity.
> The benefits of an extended education are, if the
> women chooses to be a full-time housewife rather
> than continue in employment, merely deflected
> from her previous occupation to her equally import-
> ant new occupation and manifest themselves in a
> different way.

In the First Commission report there is a realism, which is
absent from the report of the Second Commission, about the
amount of work involved in rearing children and the impact
this has on income and workforce participation. They allow 'it
may well be possible' for a woman with two children or fewer to
work at least part-time 'except when the children are very young'.
But their chief concern is the family of three children or more,
whose mother will usually be working in the home or whose
childcare requirements would be very great if she did not. While
they advocate the introduction of equal pay, they want society

to find a way to adjust the income of those with major family responsibilities.

People forget that the argument for paying men more than women was that men were more likely to be providing for a family. The First Commission argued that this was not always true and even when it was it was plainly unfair. Few people today would disagree with them. What seems to have been lost, however, is the First Commission's understanding that society has a duty to provide directly for some of the cost of rearing a family or single-income families will not be able to compete.

The First Commission suggested what was in effect a payment to mothers at home: an allowance to families in which there was a child under five, or, if there were two or more children, the youngest was under seven. This was to be phased in with the introduction of equal pay. It never was. Second Commission-member, economist and mother-of-six Finola Kennedy suggests that this was partly the reason that Charles Haughey charged the Second Commission with revisiting the issue of women in the home.

And although child benefit had been paid directly to mothers since 1974 (by which time it was in practice paid to mothers in 80 per cent of cases) the Second Commission recommended against any increase in child benefit: 'Such investment is better directed to specific supports for low-income families, towards supports for childcare and eldercare and towards education and training opportunities for women.'

In other words, women were not to be supported to care for their own children but *not* to care for them.

Finola Kennedy found herself out of tune with the Commission on these issues and others. She says that a couple of people on the Commission came to her and said they would support her if she wrote a Minority Report. She decided to do it on her own so as not to 'fracture' the committee. She begins:

The contents of this Minority Report are strongly influenced by the voices of women as expressed in the written submissions, oral presentations and informal contacts. If these expressions had to be summarised briefly, the message would be, that while many women have found a voice and greater public recognition in the form of pay, status and other rewards, there are very many other women who are receiving little or only token recognition. The latter include, in particular, women caring for their families and communities, and engaged in a vast amount of voluntary work, without which the state itself could not survive.

Her focus on the importance of the care of young children is up-to-the-minute:

While caring for children may be approached from the viewpoint of the restraints on freedom which it places on the carer, it is hardly necessary to state that caring for children, one's own and others, affords tremendous potential for human fulfilment. The acquisition of language, the development of motor skills, the growth from dependence to independence are areas of study which command considerable intellectual prestige. Yet it is not by accident that the first language learnt is called 'the mother tongue'. Everyone who cares for a child is directly engaged in this great laboratory of childhood.'

She makes a strong case for parents having the choice to care for their children at home and argues for child benefit to be doubled – and taxed if necessary. She has got her way on the first count and may yet on the second.

Asked now why the Second Commission could not come with her on this, she says, 'I suppose they didn't want to be too supportive of women in the home. Because that would be being supportive of something which was keeping women back.' She thinks also that she was pigeonholed as a Catholic: 'I'd say they thought I was from the backwoods.'

The strong focus of the Second Commission on access to paid work as an index of equality has followed through into much of the work of the National Women's Council of Ireland. One of their most recent reports, on pensions, takes this ideology to an extreme. It states baldly that although periods of care should be recognised, this should not 'lock women into long-term patterns of caring'.

Where they want to go is towards a 'carer worker' society, in which there is no gender difference in participation in paid work. This could be achieved by everyone working three-quarter jobs. Men are to be 'socially constructed' as carers; women are to be 'socially constructed' as workers.

I don't know about you but I don't want to be 'socially constructed' by anyone. The tone adopted reminds me of that of a missionary entering an unknown culture with a vision of making it just like his own.

I have come to believe that the challenge for society is not to 'socially construct' sameness but to accept diversity. Even if 95 per cent of the carers of babies on the road are women, we should equally accept the 5 per cent who are men. Even if 80 per cent of those picking up schoolgoing children at the gate are women, we should equally accept the 20 per cent who are men.

This is a much more interesting challenge than calling for a fifty-fifty ratio of men and women in caring and employment roles, particularly as, unlike the fifty-fifty ratio idea, it has some chance of being realised.

4

## We Shall Not Conceive:
## What Our Mothers Taught Us

*Mother is the dead heart of the family, spending father's earnings on consumer goods to enhance the environment in which he eats, sleeps and watches television…*
                                        Germaine Greer, *The Female Eunuch*

My mother spent the nine months of her pregnancy with me crying. She was forty-two and absolutely horrified. She thought her family was complete after my brother and sister were born, seventeen and fourteen years before. She had been practising contraception but obviously practice did not make perfect.

To add insult to injury, as she told the actress Rosaleen Linehan, she had just bought a white carpet.

She was also completely terrified that I would be disabled. One night when I was in my twenties and she had had a few drinks, she waved her cigarette at me and commented to my sister that I hadn't turned out too badly considering, 'She could have been a Mongol.' Instead, as a friend responded drily, I turned out to be Irish.

For my mother, who had third-level education, whose parents had third-level education and who was Protestant to boot, control of her fertility was absolutely central to her sense of herself. She was ahead of the posse. This equation of fertility control with status and possibility was common throughout the western world but like most things except rain took longer to reach Ireland.

'We shall not, we shall not conceive,' sang the journalist Mary Kenny to the tune of 'We Shall Not be Moved' outside the Dáil on the occasion of Mary Robinson's attempt to get a reading of her contraception bill in 1971. When I read this my first reaction is to shudder at her insensitivity to the many, many women who *can't* conceive. There's a long, fascinating distance between Mary Kenny in 1971 and me in 2010. She was twenty-seven. She was probably too young to know anyone trying and failing to have a baby. Her focus was on access to contraception. I have had access to contraception right through my fertile life.

Some Irish feminists try to pretend that women's problems are still the same, that the 'movement' still has the same aims. Much like hard-line Irish republicans throw a line back to Pearse and then forward, insisting that progress must be made along that line.

But we are not leaders of a movement or custodians of a tradition. We are seeking here to articulate honestly where Irishwomen are now, particularly as mothers. When we throw the line backwards, it loops and even breaks.

When I meet Mary Kenny now she makes clear to me the extent to which access to contraception has changed motherhood: 'Contraception changed everything,' she says. 'In pre-contraception times, people just regarded children as a hazard of life. That was Princess Anne's phrase – 'a hazard of marriage'. Once you choose to have a child, it becomes a conscious choice and a responsibility. You can't say, "God sent them, I've nothing to do with it." She uses an expression which sums up the dour resignation with which children were regarded by some – "the will of God". Why does this remind me of the tone of the National Women's Council's description of caring for children: 'a burden, a source of fulfilment or a complex combination of the two...'

She points out that the post-contraception baby boom now taking place in Ireland is unique in Europe: 'When women have choices and they're able to have children they *like* having children.'

According to Eurostat, in 2009 Ireland had the highest birth rate in the EU: 16.8 per 1000, as against an average of 10.7, followed by the UK at 13, France at 12.9 and Estonia at 12.2.

The lowest rate was in Germany (8.3) while Malta, Austria and Bulgaria came next (9.2).

'More Irish women are choosing to have children,' reported the *Irish Independent* on 5 September 2009. 'The career women of the 1980s have given way to the noughties woman who wants to have it all, including a family. She was having 2.1 children, on average, up from 2.0 the year before, and 1.9 the year before that. This was not a scenario that anyone among the social scientists, statisticians or feminists foresaw.'

It would surely be hard for this generation of new mothers to understand fully the struggle for contraceptive rights in this country. When Mary Kenny was singing outside the Dáil it was illegal to sell condoms and the Pill was prescribed as a 'period regulator'. However, I imagine that the biggest differences between then and now are not legal but emotional and psychological.

Kenny writes in *Woman x Two: How to Cope with a Double Life* (1978) of the social and psychological restrictions placed on girls of her generation:

> Girls, from an early age, were very firmly kept in line. They were generally made to work harder around the home than boys. They were less well educated. They were imbued with a strong sense of responsibility about their duties to their families and to society. And a firm lid was kept on their sexuality. This was done by greatly emphasising, to girls, the overriding value of chastity outside marriage and of submission within it. Any girl who transgressed these social laws paid a great price. An unmarried pregnant girl was, habitually, put on the boat to America if she lived on the west coast and to England if she lived on the east. My mother remembers unmarried girls who became pregnant simply drowning themselves.

A friend's older sister – of the Kenny generation – was driven from Waterford to the mail boat in Dún Laoghaire and sent to England in the early stages of pregnancy.

By the 1980s the social climate had radically changed. The story of my friend's sister, when told to me, seemed quite unbelievable. It is clear, in hindsight, that although we associate the 1980s with the religious fervour of the anti-divorce and anti-amendment campaigns, these were symptoms of dissolution, not of resurgence. Although it is true that in the 1980s, when I was in my teens, there was still a legal ban on the sale of condoms and the Pill except as a 'period regulator', at least in Dublin this had become a joke: everyone knew where you bought condoms and doctors freely prescribed the Pill. Remember the one about the man going into the Virgin Megastore in Dublin wanting a Daniel O'Donnell album, who's so embarrassed at the till that he asks for a packet of condoms?

When the law changed in 1985 it seemed like a technicality to me and my friends. Although many factors were at play in that change (increasing globalisation, education, entry into the EU) much credit for it must go to the very women's movement of which Mary Kenny was a part in the early 1970s.

But I think it is the psychological change that is most interesting. Sure, having the technical devices which prevent pregnancy is important but feeling you have the right to use them is more so. The availability of the devices informed that sense of having a right but so did factors such as education and the possibility of economic independence.

We have to understand not just the lack of access to contraceptive devices that affected women of a previous generation but what it must have been like to feel you did not have the right to control your fertility. It was terrifying. It was destabilising. And we must understand that it was this horror that informed Irish feminism of the 1970s.

I have to get my head around the fears women had then, says journalist Nell McCafferty, a key member of Irish Women's Liberation Movement: 'The fear of what society would do to you if you got pregnant. Don't forget the Magdalen homes. The fear, as Nuala Fennell says, of "unremitting pregnancy". We thought we could solve it with contraception. Of course you can solve a lot with that. But the second issue was earning your own money. Remember the marriage bar. You couldn't even collect the children's allowance. Women didn't have money.'

I tell her I remembered none of it. It was history.

'You know your history but at that point we were living it,' she says.

'We forget our history at our peril,' wrote journalist Mary Holland in *The Irish Times* in 1999, during the hoo-haa over tax individualisation. I worked with Mary Holland and I loved her: she was brilliant, kind, gentle and fair. However, even then, I was stunned by this reactionary statement. If it had come out of the mouth of a loyalist or a republican in the North, Holland would surely have seen it as reactionary. But the women's revolution was her revolution.

The strong lesson of that history to a young woman is – metaphorically – to keep her legs together. Pregnancy is greatly feared, not now because of society's censure but because of its cost to a woman's economic independence. The importance of this independence and the fear of its loss are made paramount in a woman's life; the loss of emotional contact is downplayed. You could almost say that the need for economic success simply replaced moral censure (in itself an economic mechanism) as the reason women feared pregnancy. This is what not forgetting history has meant to women of my generation.

I went to Nell McCafferty for a fix on how we got where we are because I knew from her writing that she never stops questioning. We spent five hours thrashing through where she was then and where we were now over cups of tea in her Dublin home.

'We always forget history at our peril,' she says, when I mention Mary Holland's comment in *The Irish Times* to her. 'So in the North, for instance, should we just go on and on nursing our grievances?

Of course not, she says; but in the context of women she fears that if we go soft on our advance on the workplace 'they' will send us 'back to the kitchen sink'.

'No, they won't do that.'

'Will they not?'

I told her I thought the 'they' she was talking about was about as real as the bogeyman. That instead there had been a massive campaign at the highest level of get women out of their homes and into the workplace. That it was all about economics and it had always been about economics. Betty Friedan had brilliantly shown how advertisers colluded to make American women stay at home in the 1950s so that they would buy more stuff but now it was in advertisers' interests to keep women working.

As the recession has deepened, I have reflected again on McCafferty's fears. Now I think it is possible that retiring women from the workforce will be seen by some economists as a clever way of sharing out the unemployment that will result not just from the financial collapse but from the exhaustion of natural resources. But I think it will be cleverer for women to fight for proper reward for caring work than to fight the men for work outside the home, if they do not, at that particular stage in their lives, want it.

Being forced to continue to work full-time through your children's young lives if you don't want to is no fun, as McCafferty agrees: 'When I came back from Canada [in the 1970s] I said, "Jesus, now a woman has two jobs. In the home and outside it." And mortgages…first I think women actually wanted to work outside the home but then came mortgages so you had no choice, hardly.'

She says she could see 'trouble ahead' in the dual career life of Canadian couples but she didn't know what to do about it and 'no one was listening anyway'.

'There's a part of me says if you go to all that effort to make a baby and that's such a bloody wonder of nature, why wouldn't you stay at home for two years and enjoy the baby and give it the best? Could we not turn this thing around? But to do that I lose promotion. I mightn't get my job back. Over to you, guys.'

I tell her of Labour TD Eithne Fitzgerald's wonderful 2002 plan to guarantee women their jobs back after three years' parental leave.

'Now, Eithne, how do they get their job back? I'm a reasonable person. You've lost three years' experience. You're going to the back of the queue, sister.'

What concerns her is the post-recession reality. She keeps pulling me up with the word, 'Yesterday'.

'Yesterday,' she says, 'the parent at home was not discussed openly. The climate was inhospitable. The current disadvantage can be turned to an advantage *if it is handled properly*. We'll all go to the kitchen sink for a while and we'll realise isn't it great to be off the treadmill. Isn't it great to actually enjoy parenting? Isn't it great for the children? And we will have a choice to go out to work again. But we have to keep the possibility of choice open.'

I tell her I think the issue is not whether a woman is in the home or not but whether this disadvantages her or not. Why shouldn't she be paid? She asks the wholly valid question: who will pay for this? 'I'm agreeing we tax the fuckers, every penny off Bono, Mr Smurfit, the lot. Sack half the public service. It still isn't enough. You're a productive individual, you're raising children, you should be paid. You've a hell of a sell on your hands.'

The truth is that I have not thought clearly about the implications of not having economic independence within a marriage or partnership because I can't imagine it. When I married I was working outside the home and earning more than my husband. I continued to work outside the home until I saw fit to stop. I know my value in the marketplace and for this reason I can accurately assess my value in the home.

I am educated, have experience and could find work again although I might never equal the income I had ten years ago. Why does this not bother me? I suppose because I share equally with my husband in his income and believe I earn it as much as he does. Obviously, he would not be able to do the kind of work he does outside the home if I didn't work in it. Obviously, the most important work we are doing as a family is raising the children.

This wasn't always obvious to me, however. I remember in my early days as a journalist I interviewed the Muslim owner of a Pakistani take-away. I asked him if his wife was at home full-time in order to tick the box 'conservative values' and no doubt endear myself further to the sisterhood. What he said knocked me for six:

'She does the important work, raising the children. I just bring home the bacon.'

Of course, it is crucial for the male partner to see it this way if the female homemaker is to feel valued and economically viable. My husband always has. But recently two of my friends had incidents with their husbands when they pulled rank because they 'earn' more money. In one case if was just a husband's throw-away comment that his wife was 'reluctant to spend my money.'

He has since given up his job and she is supporting the family.

In the other case it was more serious: a fight about whether a paint colour should be changed ended with his words: 'I want it changed. I'm paying for it.' My friend didn't talk to her husband for days. It's not surprising she has no plan to give up her part-time work and is keen to ratchet it up as soon as possible.

It is, I think, more likely to be confidence in her relationship than subservience and conditioning that allows a woman to depend financially on a man. Catherine Hakim reports that, in the US, black women are more likely to remain financially independent within marriage than white women.

I do not feel my equality within my relationship is threatened by the fact that I earn next to no money. 'I go into the home as an equal,' as I put it to Nell McCafferty.

'Are you saying you have completely equal access to the income?'

'Yes.'

'You have a joint bank account?'

'Yes.'

'All the money goes there?'

'Yes.'

'But he can at any stage revoke that.'

'He wouldn't.'

'But he could. I'm talking about the law.'

'Well, then, I would walk.'

It is true that as things stand in Ireland (and all other common-law countries) the primary carer has no legal right to a portion of the assets during the life of the relationship. Fundamentally, she depends on the earner's goodwill, although it is likely that without that goodwill she would not be living with him. It is also possible that, without that goodwill, she would walk and that the law would eventually support her in a division of the assets. But, asks Nell McCafferty, how easy is it to walk out of a marriage, particularly if you have children?

She has a point. The carer in the home is economically disadvantaged in a relationship. I would make the case for a radical redistribution of income from earners to carers: a legal right to an equal share of the assets during a marriage and high, taxed child benefit to bump up the income of couples on low wages.

Others want high taxes and institutional childcare so that women can work outside the home to achieve an equal income. I think the price, for women and children, is too high. Meanwhile, I would not recommend to my daughter to live her life according to the assumption that men are not to be trusted.

Their personal histories have informed the life's work of our founding feminists, just as my history informs my work. Mary Kenny writes in *Woman x Two* of the fact that many of the founding mothers of Irish liberation 'rebelled' out of resentment at how their fathers had treated their mothers.

'What do you earn, Hugh?' Nell McCafferty still remembers the question her mother asked her father. 'She never knew what he earned,' she says. 'He'd say, "Don't you worry, if there's an emergency I've a little something set aside."'

There is obviously nothing wrong with the fact that women were reacting against the dynamics of their own families when they took up feminism: these dynamics were reflections of the dynamics of society. But each story had its own individual twists and the problem for me and women of my generation was that so many of our feminist role models had extremely negative experiences of family from which some of them extrapolated a world view. Wrongs had to be righted and some of these wrongs were men who were controlling and violent, whether they were fathers or partners. Small wonder that we tended to see liberation in terms of escape from our families of origin and from family in general.

My own life experience was completely different. My father, Jack White, was a sweetheart. He never seemed to question the innate equality of women (interestingly, neither does my father-in-law, and my husband's conditioning in this regard is probably one of the main reasons I married him). It's not surprising that it never occurred to me to question my ability to follow any career I wanted.

My mother didn't work outside the home. She never wanted to. What she loved was being at home, creating her amazing garden. Looking back, it's true that my father had access to money in a way she didn't. She had to ask for money while he didn't. Also, working as one of the founder executives in RTÉ television, he had the freedom to travel at will and meet countless interesting people, which she didn't have – and didn't seem to want.

There were ways in which she was not equal, then, but she certainly thought she was equal. To be perfectly honest there were ways in which he was not equal, either, like having to bear the lifelong yoke of providing for us. But he thought he was equal too.

He brought her breakfast in bed every morning, gave me my breakfast and got me out to school. I remember, as a child, sitting at a neighbour's table when the father asked me to pour him a cup of tea. I stared at the teapot in disbelief. It was equidistant between him and me. I reviewed the degree of expertise required to pour tea. And I am glad to say that I told him to pour it himself.

I would be an angrier woman today if I had had that father. But being asked to pour a cup of tea is a far cry from the kind of indignity to which some fathers subjected their families. Nuala O'Faolain's memoir, *Are You Somebody?*, was an international bestseller. Its picture of a philandering, alcoholic father and a crushed mother obviously struck a chord.

There is a passage in that book which I doubt anyone who read it can ever forget:

> Once, when my father had gone down the country on a job, she broke the unwritten rules by daringly going into Dublin, and going to Kingsbridge station, and surprising him by being at the barrier when he got off the train. He was with people. He leaned down to aim a kiss at her cheek before hurrying off with them. 'He didn't even take the cigarette out of his mouth,' she told me, not once, but over and over again, in years to come.
>
> I imagine her making her lonely way back to us children. She was still in her twenties. She would have taken the bus out to the terminus, then walked out past the last street-lamp, then down the dark country road to the estate's gate-lodge, then ducked under a fence and followed the path we'd worn in the tussocky field across to the bungalow...Nothing there but children.

It is not surprising that she and other women with similar childhoods put such emphasis, not just on contraception but on paid work. Nor is it surprising that O'Faolain didn't have children herself. She was not brought up to value children and was not valued herself as a child. She didn't need me to point out that it was her own unmet needs as a child that led her, in her sixties, to the overwhelming jealousy of her new partner's child described in *Almost There: the Onward Journey of a Dublin Woman*.

Although Nuala O'Faolain's story contained certain central truths that struck a chord with thousands, her story was extreme. As a young woman, reading her columns through the 1980s and 1990s, I understood her voice to be that of a calm, measured, middle-aged commentator. But she was damaged enough to have in her the capacity for this extreme reaction to an eight-year-old child. It's not her fault that she had the reaction but that she chose to publicise it to her readers makes me sick. For the sake of her own expiation, or whatever, hatred of a child became public to thousands and eventually, necessarily, to the child herself.

When I was growing to maturity, I did not see the feminist opinion-makers which formed me as being part of the social history of the country. I viewed them as revolutionary leaders are typically viewed, as having no history and no social context. But of course women now in their sixties and seventies were part of a society which not only gave women little autonomy in their sexual and professional lives but valued children very little. These women were bound to be affected by that view. As Ireland becomes more affluent and more educated and people have fewer children than in the pre-contraceptive era, women are surely understanding and valuing their children more and more.

This is one of the reasons why they are not all following the path prepared for them by the previous generation of feminists. Their torch gives them a wider field of vision.

The journalist June Levine was a central figure in the original Women's Liberation Movement and she was also its first historian, in her book *Sisters*. It's a great read but breathtaking in the bitterness and anger it displays. Levine describes marriage as 'another word for slavery' and working in the home is described as 'the housewife's cage'. Towards the end there's a scene in which she reports the drama of her daughter's announcement that she is getting married, describing it as 'this suicidal attempt on her own identity'.

Throughout the text of *Sisters*, 'work' is always a great thing, as long as it is not work in the home. Levine is typical of her generation in thoroughly confusing caring for children with housework and, most depressingly, servicing a patriarch. This is how she describes the work of the house which she wants men to share:

> Nowadays I realise that men can also feed children,
> wash clothes, scour cookers, do shopping, scrub the
> loos, make decisions as to what to have for dinner,

drop kids off in playschool, pick 'em up again, fill my
chest of drawers with clean knickers, bras and tights
as surely as I have always done for them. The game's
up as far as male chauvinism is concerned and I can't
understand how any conscious young woman can
rationalise the song-and-dance routine of bygone
days.

In this account the rearing of children is confined to the
provision of food and transport and more or less equated with
filling the knickers' drawer. Fascinatingly, Nell McCafferty also
focuses on underwear, when discussing women's role in the home
with me: 'I would love to get up in the morning and have clean
knickers ready for me.'

There is a chasm between my expectations of marriage and
those of Levine's generation but even for her generation, Levine's
experience of marriage was far from typical. The extremeness
of her opinions on marriage must have derived to a large extent
from her horrific marriage breakdown. Married to a Canadian
doctor at nineteen, she emigrated there with him and suffered
the classic Betty Friedan-style isolated housewife's role, complete
with a serious nervous breakdown. She came home to Ireland
to recuperate with her two children and had her marriage
terminated by telegram from Canada.

She was not the first woman to suffer a terrible marriage
breakdown and she won't be the last. But to extrapolate from her
own experience to generalise about all marriages was unwise. It is
true that forces were working against women in marriages in the
1950s: lack of financial independence; lack of education; lack of
proper protection in the case of marital breakdown; and domestic
violence. But many women negotiated terms with their husbands
with which they were very happy.

Whether marriage itself was to be condemned or whether it
was to be renegotiated was the argument which caused a very
public rift in the Irish Women's Liberation Movement, when
Nuala Fennell resigned. The occasion of Nuala Fennell's resig-

nation from the movement, on 19 June 1971, was its opposition to the Forcible Entry and Occupation Bill but her letter
of resignation clearly shows deeper disagreement: 'At a recent
seminar,' she wrote, 'it was clearly stated that if any member,
whatever her previous views, was not against the aforementioned
Bill, then she was not in Women's Lib, and to that I can add
authoritatively that if you are not anti-American, anti-clergy,
anti-government, anti-ICA, anti-police, anti-men, then, sisters,
there is no place for you either.'

Fennell was very much an establishment figure as I was
maturing, a Fine Gael TD for Dublin South from 1981 to 1987
and 1989 to 1992 and Minister of State for Women's Affairs from
1982 to 1987. However, when I recently began to reread history,
I thought Nuala Fennell's the most practically useful voice to
emerge from the Irish Women's Liberation Movement. I wrote to
her and pretty much begged for an interview in the summer of
2009. She said she thought the book was 'a very good idea' but was
too busy finishing her autobiography.

I didn't know that she was terminally ill. She died in August of
the same year.

Her death underlined for me the importance of assessing the
history of women's liberation in Ireland now, while witnesses are
still alive.

What distinguishes Fennell, it seems to me, is how much she
likes men and given that most women do too, this is important.
Not only that: she promoted, not the abandonment of marriage
but its renegotiation, which was surely what most women wanted.

Granted, the Irish Women' s Liberation Movement's founding
text, *Chains or Change?* (1971) made a very convincing case for
avoiding marriage altogether but Nuala Fennell saw the reality
that most Irish women's lives would be lived within marriage.
She founded AIM in 1972 to fight for legal changes to make
women more equal within marriage. In *Irish Marriage: How are
You? (1974)*, she voiced an intelligent aspiration, which has, to a
large extent, come to pass: 'The ultimate objective should be the
extended education of a woman so that perhaps our daughters

may aspire to a marriage freely entered into for the best reasons and not consider it a conventional inevitability or an easy meal ticket for life.'

What had me punching the air of the National Library was this book's open and compassionate understanding that sexual repression – which was one Irish response to a history of poverty – had caused much of the 'excessive drinking, brutality, infidelity, impotence' which made misery of so many marriages. One woman whose letter is quoted in *Irish Marriage: How are You?* would take a couple of tablets and sleep in the bath if her husband had been out drinking, to avoid being beaten up. She was still a virgin.

'On the question of education,' writes Fennell, 'virtually everyone who has gone through the Irish educational system has been emotionally stunted by our repressive attitudes to sex.' Surely this included the leaders of the Irish Women's Liberation Movement?

The book is very clear about the still unresolved problem of the parent in the home having a legal right to a portion of her partner's income and it is a shame that the whole 'working woman' agenda virtually obliterated this argument for women of my generation. 'A woman,' write Fennell, 'becomes a financial cripple when she becomes a mother, she needs protection, support and an understanding that should match the priceless job she is doing. Her status in this country is unjustifiable.'

That said, Fennell's memoir, *Political Woman*, published posthumously in 2009, shows her to have had the stereotypical views of success and fulfilment typical of feminists of her generation – which did not include parenting children. Either she believed in creating good conditions for women who, unlike her, would not 'succeed', or she believed in children constituting a short break in a career. Like most of her feminist colleagues who were mothers, she was at home in her children's early years. She never had to ask herself the really hard questions like, 'When is it OK for me to leave my small baby and for how long?' These are the questions that have tortured my generation.

In Fennell's memoir her description of her life at home with three small children is wholly negative: 'I felt invisible, irrelevant and in a role from which I wanted to escape.' She talks slightingly of coffee mornings and dreary trips to the supermarket and breathes a sigh of relief when she goes to a IWLM meeting and no one mentions 'children or cleaning the oven'.

Follow most Irish feminists to their source and you find Betty Friedan's *The Feminine Mystique* (1962). Nuala Fennell writes of it being read by thousands of Irish housewives when it became available in Ireland in 1970. Friedan is name-checked by most of the feminists I read or interviewed and Nell McCafferty describes joining Friedan and Bella Abzug at the United Nations Conference on Women in Copenhagen in 1980 as sitting 'at the altar of the goddesses'.

Friedan has ascended into the stratosphere to the point that you don't even have to say what she stood for any longer because people think they know. But I had to understand her to understand the generation of Irish feminists before me. Through them, she had a massive impact on me and women of my generation and the least I could do was go and read what she actually wrote.

I found *The Feminine Mystique* anchored firmly in the cultural context of its time. For instance, was it the great Friedan who said that male homosexuality was 'spreading like a murky smog' over America due to women's over-investment in mothering? And who blamed jobless housewives for causing their children's psychiatric disorders and even autism?

It is very easy to poke fun at this distance, of course, and Friedan could not have thought, as most of us do now, that homosexuals are born, not made, and that they're fine the way they are. Nor could she know that autism seems to be due, overwhelmingly, to genetic factors. She wrote *The Feminine Mystique* fifty years ago and the book has all the signs of it.

She was also writing entirely for her own social class. Her vision of success is exclusively middle-class. It makes me cringe to read: 'There is something less than fully human in those who have never known a commitment to an idea…'. It makes you see the cultural origins of our limited concept of success.

Her argument applied much more to America than it ever did to Ireland. What she described was the phenomenon of American women in the post-war period marrying very young and investing themselves wholly in home and family. By the end of the 1950s the average marriage age in the US had dropped to twenty and was still dropping. Fourteen million American women were engaged by the age of seventeen. By the mid-1950s, 60 per cent of women dropped out of college to marry, or because they didn't want too much education to put off potential husbands.

These are ghastly statistics, particularly when you consider Friedan's master stroke, which was to prove that these women were led into this lifestyle by the concerted power of advertisers. She actually spoke to advertisers who explained to her the importance of keeping women at home so that they would buy more things for their home. They could be safely encouraged to go out and work part-time – to help them buy more – but only if the 'pattern of happiness through things' were established early enough.

This discovery, probably the earliest and clearest articulation of the power of advertising, is just as relevant today as it was then. But Friedan's remedy for the women of her time was: 'a no-nonsense nine-to-five' job, an expression that comes back to me when I remember babies crying, toddlers clinging and dinner waiting to be made when I returned from my own 'no-nonsense' job. She didn't have a clue because she had never done it. Of course she'd been at home while her children were young.

(Presumably it was the 'less than human' women with no ideas who were to provide the 'good, full-time help' which was to make the professional women's lives so easy.)

Everything happened much later in Ireland. In 1963, the average age of women when they got married was twenty-seven. It did not fall to the mid-twenties until 1980, when it started to rise again. Most Irish women didn't have the disposable income to buy fully into the consumerist lifestyle of the American housewife of the 1950s and 1960s. It is only since the 1980s that we have had control over our own fertility, equal pay and our first access to high levels of disposable income for large numbers of people.

It's not surprising that Irish feminism became compacted with free-market capitalism to produce a particularly strong form of what Betty Friedan called 'the feminist mystique'. Because, unlike many of our official feminists, Betty Friedan returned to the territory of *The Feminine Mystique* after twenty years and thoroughly questioned its assumptions. I had always heard that *The Second Stage* was a slightly embarrassing 'recantation' of Friedan's earlier work but it is nothing of the kind: it is a version of the argument that evolved in the light of changing times. But evolving arguments, honest about their own limitations within their time and place, do not make good founding texts of revolutionary movements. As far as Irish revolutionary feminism was concerned, Betty was to stay as she was.

Betty had other ideas. In *The Second Stage* she wrote: 'I think we must at least admit and begin to openly to discuss feminist denial of the importance of family, of women's own needs to give and get love and nurture, tender loving care.'

# 5

# The Mammy War

*The divide is not between parents who choose to stay at home and those who choose to go to work. Instead, there is a gap between the government, which wishes to maximise participation in the workforce and the majority of parents, who believe the ideal childcare arrangement is with parents in the home.*

Roger Jupp, Managing Director of Lansdowne
Market Research, commenting on his poll on parenting
in *The Irish Examiner*, 9 November 2005

It was 2005, the year in which a full-scale ideological war went on in Irish society about how we should rear our children. Ireland was in the full frenzy of its boom. This was the point at which we had money and could actually decide what to do with it. It was the moment when, it seemed to some, we could go the way of the Danes, build a state childcare system and get the mammies out to work.

I entered the fray that May when John Minihan, education spokesperson of the junior coalition partner in government, the Progressive Democrats, issued a proposal for schools to be kept open from 7am to 7pm to offer 'wrap-around' childcare. Nothing would do me but to burst into print, so I lobbed in an article to the opinion page of *The Irish Times*, which, in fairness, continues to offer space to divergent views: It appeared on 10 May.

How can Progressive Democrat spokesman on education John Minihan describe his childcare policy as

'child-centred' as he did in this paper last Tuesday? If it were a child-centred policy it would include parents. Children tend to really like their parents. Parents tend to really like their children. It's nature's idea of a child-centred childcare policy.

Only when you banish parents does childcare became a 'problem' to be 'tackled' rather than a joyously challenging part of being human.

In Sweden, where generous parental leave is offered as well as institutional childcare, nearly all parents take the leave. But Minihan's policy is concerned solely with making paid, formal childcare more available. It includes no measures to allow parents more choice to care for their own children.

It's pretty much forbidden to mention such fripperies under the present government. A concerted attempt to provide for paid parental leave was recently thrown out by the Department of Finance.

Fifteen other EU countries have paid parental leave, seven of them for three years. Three of the remaining six have a statutory right to part-time work. But for our government, the problem with parents as minders is the perceived cost.

The comparison even with Britain is shocking. There, the Childcare Commission, which reported to government in 2001, concerned itself as much with support for parents as for paid childcare. Because it reported potential damage to a child if his or her mother returned to work within the first year, paid maternity leave was extended to twelve months. We get eighteen weeks. Because it focused on children's need to be with their parents, part-time work became a legal right for parents of young children. We can sing for it.

It recognised that in a two-income society,

parents need direct financial support in their children's needy early years. A tax-related and so means-tested payment for parents of children under three was proposed, which could fund parents to stay at home or be passed on to a crèche or child minder.

By contrast, Minihan baldly suggests tax relief against childcare costs, which benefits only working parents. As far back as 1998, the Commission on the Family rejected the idea of tax relief on childcare as inequitable. They suggested tax individualisation and proposed instead a new direct payment to the stay-at-home parent of a child under three. Charlie McCreevy name-checked the Commission as he introduced tax individualisation. But he left out the parents' payment.

Increased child benefit, neither taxed nor targeted, can't begin to make up the income lost by parents of pre-school children.

The attack on parenting led by this government is aided by ignorance, wilful or otherwise, of recent research into child psychology. Surely Minihan must have consulted the report of the British Childcare Commission? Maybe not, for he proposed that schools stay open from 7 am to 7 pm, if necessary.

Under the heading, 'Some children are not happy in childcare,' the British report says: 'There are also some issues concerning childcare arrangements using school facilities as it is often seen as an extension of school.'

It is shameful that the report of the National Childcare Strategy (1999) confined its research into group care for children aged from three to six. The negative research findings for children in group care nearly all relate to the under-threes and particularly the under-twos.

Child psychologist Penelope Leach, co-director since 1998 of the largest-ever UK study into childcare, Families, Children and Childcare, told the *Guardian*, 'It is fairly clear from data from different parts of the world that the less time children spend in group care before three years the better.'

Why then is the government committed to creating childcare places for one in three of the under-threes by 2010? Why then, when part-time group care seems to be associated with few negative research findings, is the government actively discouraging it in favour of full-time places? Because the government cares about women's earning power and not about children.

A few days later *The Marian Finucane Show* asked me to go on to talk about childcare. My friends said not to do it, because I would be 'set up'. Indeed I thought it had to be a set-up because what I had written was not, I thought, controversial enough to merit the airtime. But I agreed to do it because I believed what I had said and was prepared to defend it.

The show's researcher spoke to me with a tone of suppressed incredulity, as if she was going to break out into hysterical laughter as soon as she put down the phone. I could not fathom what I had said that was so outrageous as to shock her so much. What I found out when I went on air on 25 May 2005 was that it was not anything I had actually said but something I was imagined to have said. Marian Finucane's second question – or assertion – to me on prime-time national radio was that I did not believe a father can provide care for a child because I 'figured it was a mother's natural role'.

I had never said this. So there followed a deeply embarrassing pause as I disassociated myself from these ideas and Finucane expertly changed tack. You could have cut the atmosphere with a knife during the break as it was decided to drop a man from the show – presumably a dad who had been found to disagree with me over the airwaves. From this I learned a very important lesson: it isn't what you say; it's what you're perceived to say. And in Ireland, at that time at least, saying that parents should be given the option of staying home with small children meant saying that mothers should not work outside the home because only mothers could raise their children.

On 14 January 2010 I happened to turn on the radio and heard RTÉ's Donal O'Herlihy telling Ryan Tubridy why he'd taken a two-year career break and moved to rural France. He said the decision to take the leave began to form when he was dropping his fourteen-month-old daughter into the crèche after a long weekend and felt 'the wrench'. He would sometimes excitedly tell the crèche staff that she was doing something new and then realise from their reaction that she had been doing it for ages but he wasn't around to notice. He said he was sure parents all over Ireland were going through the same experience. So he resolved to take a long break – he did not say how he funded it – and painted a picture of his current life, coming home with warm bread under his arm and seeing his daughter run up to meet him at the door.

If a woman – me, for instance – had said any of that there would have been war. I would have been dissing the crèche. I would have been saying that every other woman should give up her job when obviously it was only the likes of me who could afford to do anything of the kind.

I had become a 'transgressive' figure; I was someone who unsettled the accepted scheme of things. The crude and only partially true version of my story was that I had had a high-profile, well-paying job and that I had given it up to mind my children.

On the *Marian Finucane Show* that Saturday, Dr Evelyn Mahon, Senior Lecturer in Sociology in University College, Dublin, was also a participant. She referred to Hakim's theory of the three categories of mother and concluded: 'Victoria can now be classified as a very home-centred woman.' I'm sure my friends were choking on their toast all over Dublin.

During the break I protested at being categorised as 'home-centred'.

'That's what you are,' said Marian Finucane.

Well, there I was, firmly in my place. I felt like a species of domestic fowl.

There's no doubt but that Hakim's categorisations are a useful guide. But to apply them to explain away a person's life seems to me to be a mistake. Circumstances over which they have no control are also important forces dictating the lives of mothers.

Was I 'home-centred'? Well, hello there, I was sitting in a radio studio speaking about an article I had written for a national newspaper. Of course, my primary concern is my children but this is surely the case for most mothers. Different mothers have different opportunities. I have a passion for writing which fits comfortably into a 'home-centred' life and I have always done a lot of voluntary work. At the time of the 'home-centred' categorisation, I was dreaming up a series of cultural events for Cullenswood House, which houses my children's school. This work culminated in a book about the house which was published in 2010. I was also soon to start work as an environmental activist with Stop Climate Chaos and become co-founder of the first local branch of Friends of the Earth in the Republic.

This work was all made possible by the fact that my husband was earning enough to keep us. Had he not been, I reckon I would have been hacking away as a freelance journalist. My categorisation would then, I presume, be changed to that of 'career woman', when the only difference would have been that I was doing less interesting, less flexible work which was earning me money. Then we could all have gone home happy.

These were nuances which seemed beyond the ken of the media at the time. In the months before the budget in December 2005, the mainstream media launched a campaign for the provision of a state childcare system which would free more women to work outside the home. Presumably this was done because it was felt that this was what people wanted – and indeed some people did want it.

But it also seemed as if the agenda was partly coming from the media people themselves. We saw in Catherine McGuinness's discussion how trade unionists and employers exerted a powerful influence on the Second Commission for the Status of Women. In the same way media organisations consist exclusively of employed people and they tend to reflect the interests of these people.

I should know. I was one of them.

*The Irish Times* ran what seemed to me an intense campaign on this issue, although, a campaign probably looks intense only if you don't agree with it. I cheered along with the other intense campaigns I remember, on divorce back in the 1980s, and for a 'yes' vote on the Lisbon Treaty in 2008 and 2009 but if you were on the other side of the fence, *The Irish Times* was uncomfortable reading.

This time I was sitting on the fence and even on the other side of it. It wasn't a nice place to be, particularly as, it seemed, I was on a different side from most of my former colleagues, some of them friends. However, as Mary Robinson said on RTÉ's *Would You Believe?* documentary last year in relation to the disapproval of her family when she championed contraceptive rights in Ireland in the 1970s, when you stand up for something, 'You have to be prepared to pay the price.'

Bang, bang, bang, went *The Irish Times* campaign. On 7 September the news pages revealed that the cabinet of the Fianna Fáil/PD coalition government was close to finalising a 'comprehensive state childcare system'. The chairwoman of the National Economic and Social Forum, Maureen Gaffney, had addressed the cabinet, saying that 'we had to get away from the concept that parents were totally responsible for young children'.

More controversially, she stated that 'the argument was now settled' on whether children were harmed by being placed in childcare rather than being at home.

She told the Fianna Fáil conference: 'Irrespective of the amount of time in childcare and the age of entry the proportion of children with secure emotional attachment was exactly the same, at 62 per cent, as those reared at home by their mother.'

I remember feeling very worried when I read that phrase: 'The argument is now settled.' Surely the discussion of the impact of different approaches to childcare was just beginning? As even that proponent of maternal employment and economic growth, the OECD, points out, the research findings on non-maternal care for the under-threes are 'mixed'.

In fact the National Economic and Social Forum's own research document, 'Early Childhood Care and Education', released soon after the Fianna Fáil conference, backed up its argument for more state involvement in childcare by quoting psychologists who conclude that 'only full-time work (for the mother) up to when the child is eighteen months...has adverse effects on child cognitive development.' Another way of putting this is to say that it may damage a child's cognitive development if his or her mother goes out to work full-time before he or she is a year and a half old.

That's three of my four beauties. And worse for me, the same research suggests that the more educated the mother, the more 'disadvantaged' a child is by maternal employment. In other words, the more educated you are the more your child may miss out by not having you around when he or she is very small.

An entirely different use could have been made of this research – to push for a year and a half's leave for all mothers, for instance, or a legal right to part-time work for part of that period. But this did not suit the economic or social climate of the time. The focus was firmly on jobs for the girls.

Given the pressures under which journalists and their editors operate, it is reasonable to assume that Gaffney's argument to the Fianna Fáil conference was simplified in the report in *The Irish Times*. Two weeks later the paper published an explanatory article by Gaffney (17 September 2005) which clarified her position by referring to the National Institute of Child Health and Development (NICHD) study in the US, which has been charting the progress of 1300 children and their families since 1991.

The clearest finding of the NICHD study on children and

childcare (www.nichd.nih.gov) seems to be that 'maternal sensitivity' – the mother's awareness of and ability to respond to her child's needs – is what matters most. Children with mothers who are aware of them in this way seem to fare very well in childcare situations; children whose mothers aren't or can't be aware of them in this way – because of depression or a myriad other factors – are put at higher risk of 'insecure attachment' to their mothers by long hours of poor-quality care.

It seems to be a vicious circle because the less aware the mother is, the more likely she is to put her children in less good quality care and for longer hours. She is also likely, as Gaffney pointed out in her article, 'to hold strong views that children benefit from maternal employment because it makes them more independent'.

This is an opinion I've often heard mothers express. It gives me the willies. The crèche owner who rang up during the *Marian Finucane Show* in which I participated pointed to the 'independence of crèche-reared children' as their main advantage over home-reared kids.

The NICHD research also contains the finding that among boys, it is those who are in non-maternal care for more than thirty hours a week who are most at risk of insecure attachment; while among girls, it is those who are in non-maternal care for *fewer* than ten hours a week.

Children who went into non-maternal care early and for long periods were more likely to be aggressive at four-and-a-half than those who didn't but these differences had disappeared by the age of nine or ten. Children who experienced non-maternal care were slightly advantaged in educational and cognitive skills but in this area, as in the area of the emotions, the home background was what really mattered. But 'the big exception' here, in Gaffney's words, were children from socio-economically disadvantaged backgrounds to whom high-quality childcare brought significant benefits in educational and cognitive development.

Different children need different things, then. This much of the argument is 'settled'.

As to how much childcare is 'safe', Gaffney is clear that this is unclear: 'The answer is that there is no scientifically established threshold.' She suggests:

> If possible, one parent should try not to work more than twenty hours a week in the first and second years and not more than thirty hours a week in the third year. For some, such a formula is neither possible nor desirable. For such parents, maximise your positive and affectionate, high-quality time with your child. Keep vigilant about signs of distress and be prepared to regularly re-examine your priorities.

All very sane advice: listen to your child and act on what you hear.

It is often necessary to simplify a message in order to lobby successfully. At this time, Maureen Gaffney was Chairwoman of the National Economic and Social Forum and she was lobbying on a series of stated policy objectives in relation to childcare, most of which were highly desirable. The NESF was looking for interventions to ensure quality in childcare and for a comprehensive pre-school system: three-and-a-half hours for every child in the year before he or she starts school. The budget of April 2009 granted them three hours.

They were also looking for a reduced pupil-teacher ratio in the infant classes, because our children can start school at the early age of four years. Holding the line on class size has, sadly, been as good as it got.

Perhaps the bald 'Childcare Pays' message was the only one that Gaffney and her colleagues thought the then government would buy. Or perhaps it was the only message the media peddled.

I stuck my neck out on the *Marian Finucane Show* and said that I thought full-time crèche care was less than optimal for babies and very small children. I think it is because of an instinct about this that nurseries and crèches rarely picture groups of babies in their publicity material but instead groups of pre-schoolers. I backed my hunch up with research but I did say that everyone will gravitate towards research which backs up their own hunches, as I have done myself.

In 2004 the first results of the largest-ever study of UK children from birth to school-age, *Families, Children and Childcare* (FCCC), became public. It was conducted under the direction of the UK's best-known child psychologist, Penelope Leach, whose no-nonsense *Your Baby and Child* guided this mammy and thousands like her through breastfeeding to tantrums and beyond. Her brilliant manifesto for children, *Children First: What Society Must Do – and Is Not Doing – for Children Today* (1994), has influenced my thinking on motherhood and children more than any other work.

Obviously I had to listen to Leach and this is what she said about the FCCC research in the *Guardian* of 8 July 2004:

> Infants spending as little as twelve hours a week in day nurseries – this is such a low threshold that it covers almost all infants in this childcare setting – showed slightly lower levels of social development and emotional regulation (less enthusiastic co-operation, concentration, social engagement and initiative) as toddlers. The tendency of government policy for more day-nursery provision to the exclusion of other types of childcare is extremely short-sighted; it's easier for an infant to catch up on cognitive skills later on, but they can't catch up on insecure attachment. The trend towards more day nurseries is out of kilter with what the research is finding.

The same *Guardian* article mentioned the research of Professor Ted Melhuish of Birkbeck College, London, described as 'probably the most respected academic in the field of childcare in the UK'. He had just completed a review of all the international research on childcare for the National Audit Office and had come to the conclusion:

> The quantity of day care under the age of two affects some aspects of social development – there's a slight risk of increased disruptive, anti-social behaviour and children less likely to obey rules and be less cooperative. You start to see it once children are spending twenty to twenty-five hours in day care and the risks increase when they are spending more than forty hours in day care, which is not atypical if the woman is in full-time employment with two commutes.

The problem with group care, Melhuish reckons, is that its 'responsiveness' is undermined by too few minders who change too often. But providing enough staff with a good enough deal to keep them in the job is so expensive that it is comparable with the cost of paying a parent to stay at home with a small child.

Marian Finucane countered my use of Leach's and Melhuish's research on air with Maureen Gaffney's analysis of the NICHD figures, as made not long before on the show. The NICHD had, she said, 'found quite the opposite'. They had found attachment in day-care-raised kids to be 'absolutely sound'.

As we have seen, this is only true for some children but it was the official line at all times in the mainstream media.

Also in September 2005, the National Women's Council launched its plan, *An Accessible Childcare Model*, which argued for a year's maternity leave, subsidised full-day care for two- and three-year-olds and subsidised after-school care for older children. This was reported exhaustively in the national media.

Few mothers would argue against longer maternity leave, more regulation of the childcare sector or, indeed, good after-school care. However, it can be argued that the report is not an objective account of how best to serve the needs of mothers and children. It is underpinned by the belief that it is not desirable for a woman to be at home full-time caring for children.

The report says: 'As family size decreases and living environments have altered, the socialisation of children outside the family circle from the age of three, and even younger, is recognised by most specialists for young children (OECD 1990).' In fact, as we have seen, the OECD reports research findings on children under three as 'mixed'. The NESF quotes research which finds against childcare for children under eighteen months. The UK government's audit of international research finds against childcare for children under eighteen months or two years. The FCCC finds against group care for children under three years. And the NICHD finds against large amounts of childcare in the early years for some children and not for others.

No doubt there is research that backs up the position of the National Women's Council but to say that it is supported by 'most specialists' is plain wrong. The report argues that the provision of a comprehensive childcare system allows for more choice. But how does cheap childcare, facilitating women to gain more financially from work outside the home, help other women to make the choice to stay at home? On the contrary, unless measures are taken to equalise their situations, it may extinguish that choice.

This argument became the central focus of a spat in *The Irish Times* on 26 September between the National Women's Council and columnist John Waters, who described the report as recommending 'the farming out of Irish children from the age of one'.

A prominently-displayed riposte from Dr Valerie Richardson, head of the School of Applied Social Science in UCD, was published in the same paper four days later, on 30 September, arguing that the provision of childcare maximises choice. She stresses the argument that increasing maternal employment leads to less child poverty. As a result of childcare provision in Denmark, she says, 'Female labour-force participation rates have increased substantially and the level of child poverty has fallen. For example, 77 per cent of mothers in Denmark are in employment and Denmark also has a child poverty rate of 2.4 per cent, the lowest of the twenty-four OECD countries. In Ireland, 53.9 per cent of mothers with one child are in employment, the percentage falling to 50.3 for mothers with second or subsequent children, while the child poverty rate is 15.7 per cent.'

Aren't we, yet again, making the assumption that the availability of childcare and maternal employment are cause and effect, while in reality a whole range of issues impacts on female employment rates, such as the traditional culture of the country, the kind of work that is available and, most of all, the availability of part-time work.

But we were not in the mood for subtleties. Right before the budget, on 3 December, the high-profile *Weekend* review in *The Irish Times* ran a top-of-the-page piece by Kate Holmquist on the Danish childcare system, entitled 'Danish Childcare a Step Ahead'. Nearly eight out of ten mothers work outside the home in Denmark, reports Holmquist, going on to quote two mothers whose children are in day care: 'Being a full-time mother by choice doesn't exist,' says Caroline. 'Why waste your education?' Her friend Mette echoes her views: 'If a mother stays at home, where is her life? What about her education? The mother would be lonely at home and the child wouldn't meet new friends, since all children are in day care.'

'The Danish system of childcare is generally regarded as the best in the world,' reports Holmquist. And there is absolutely no doubt that Denmark has a lot of which to be proud in relation to the country's care of its children, not least its low level of child poverty. One would have thought, however, that this arrangement of society in relation to children would be presented as *one* option, not as the only progressive option.

Particularly as this was not a view widely held by the Irish public. *The Irish Examiner* also gave the childcare issue blanket coverage but took a different approach. It conducted what it billed as the first nationwide opinion poll on childcare. This showed that 65 per cent of parents thought the ideal childcare arrangement was for one of them to stay at home, a situation achieved by more than half of all households with a child under fourteen. Crèche care was considered the best option by just 3 per cent of parents.

Working and stay-at-home parents were agreed that there should be more support for parenting but that it should support care by parents and care by others equally.

It seemed obvious that the *Examiner* was expecting different results. The howls for more childcare emitted by the editorial were hilariously out of tune with the results of the poll: lack of childcare was, it said, causing 'a massive loss to the labour force [that] could have devastating long-term consequences for the national economy'. It was, according to Catherine Shanahan on the front page of the paper on 9 November, 'limiting family size, forcing women to quit work and turning grandparents into unpaid child minders...' On 11 November she wrote, 'A staggering two-thirds of women are quitting full-time work once they start a family, influenced by rocketing childcare costs and inflexible working arrangements.'

She went on to detail the results of the poll in which two in three parents said that parental care was the ideal option for their children, rising to eight in ten among those who already had one parent at home. Where did the evidence of the 'limiting', the 'forcing', the 'staggering', the 'quitting' and the 'rocketing' come from?

The evidence of the poll was, however, brilliantly analysed by Harry McGee in the same newspaper on 9 November. His was a landmark piece which was very much out of tune with the song being sung from the hymn sheets of the entire media establishment at the time. What he explained was that the pressure for more childcare places, which was not strong in the country at large, was strong in the counties of the Dublin hinterland which were 'swing' constituencies' and this was why their needs were dominating public debate.

I was absolutely stunned by the article at the time, particularly the passages I quote here:

In March this year, politicians arrived from all over Ireland for canvassing duties in the Meath and Kildare North by-elections. Many discovered to their shock that they hadn't just landed in another constituency but another country.

What they witnessed was vast housing estates emptied of their people during the day; harassed young working couples rising early to beat the traffic; large chunks of family income being spent on child minders and crèches.

It wasn't that childcare wasn't on the political agenda before then. It was. The number of working mothers with children in pre-school or primary school has effectively doubled over the past twelve years to more than 400,000 (some 60,000 of them are single parents.) The government has spent €500 million on the Equal Opportunities Childcare Programme (EOCP) which has so far created 25,000 childcare places.

But the by-elections had a catalysing effect for the parties on this issue. Informed by Kildare and Meath, political responses zeroed in on the wider availability of affordable childcare in crèches and with child minders.

But the picture that emerges from the *Irish Examiner*/Lansdowne poll today is a dramatically different one, that suggests that the imperative for a decisive majority of parents is that their children be cared for by them or by other family members.

Over half of all parents with dependent children under the age of fourteen have dedicated one parent to full-time childcare. But the family connection does not stop there. One of the most intriguing findings of the poll is the role played by other family members. Extended family members (predominantly grandparents) play a role in the care of children in one in five families. This rises to a third where both parents are working full-time with children under five, even higher when the children are of primary school age.

Overall, a little over one in five uses paid private childcare, but this rises to almost 70 per cent where both parents are working and the child is under five. The latter group is comparatively small in size – some 24,000 according to the CSO survey – but most live in urban areas or in their hinterlands (and many of these will be the big swing constituencies).

Notably, the poll bears out the findings of the CSO survey on childcare, conducted in 2003, which, for the first time, identified the extent of the role played by extended family members. And while this arrangement obviously leads to cost-saving, what the poll clearly shows is that the choice is not governed by economic considerations alone.

One of the most eye-catching findings is that this arrangement is seen as a positive choice for many parents. Asked about their ideal arrangement, the most common choice for those whose children are now looked after by grandparents, uncles and aunties was that very arrangement, closely followed by the care of the parents themselves.

By marked contrast, only six per cent of the 'other family member' group identified child minder or crèche as an ideal choice, which strongly suggests that few perceive their present arrangement as an option that has been solely forced on them by the prohibitive cost of private care. People seem perfectly happy with this situation.

In an ideal world, when it comes to the conflicting choices of family versus career, there is only one clear winner.

A clear majority across all sectors would ideally

look after their own children, either full-time or part-time. But of course that is tempered by the real world. And in that world, the number of women working will increase, either to continue their careers or because both parents need to work out of necessity.

The stark evidence from the poll, however, is that the race to make more private childcare places available may be misplaced (a paltry three per cent regarding a crèche as ideal is hardly redolent of a massive desire or demand). If one was looking for policy pointers, the findings strongly trend to more family-friendly initiatives, increased maternity and parental leave; more flexible working arrangements; early education initiatives, and more financial support for both working and stay-at-home parents. Even when both parents are working, many want their child to be looked after by themselves or grandparents.

Dr Margaret Fine-Davis of the Centre for Gender and Women's Studies, Trinity College, Dublin, was asked to analyse the findings in the *Irish Examiner* on 11 November. If parents saw care by one parent at home as the ideal arrangement, it was, she said, because 'that is what they have been used to traditionally'. It was, however, 'no longer possible for most couples, because of the need for two incomes, but also because women increasingly want to use their education in the labour force.'

Hello? The poll shows that it *is* possible for a slim majority of parents to keep one parent at home. It also shows that two-thirds of parents think this is the ideal option. And why is this parental preference explained as an unthinking adherence to that most blackened of concepts, 'tradition', rather than a conscious choice?

Where is the evidence to support this interpretation?

By then *The Irish Times* was also canvassing readers' views, and on 15 November published a fascinating page of responses to Kate Holmquist's earlier series on articles on childcare, 'Who's Minding the Children?' Some voices echoed the view that childcare should be cheaper but a majority of voices called for measures to help parents have more time with their own children. A legal right to flexibility in the workplace was called for twice. Two years' paid parental leave was asked for. Banks were called on to postpone mortgage payments for parents with a child under one. One letter takes a stance which is more compelling now, from the vantage point of the recession: 'It would appear that the whole role of nurturing our children is being sacrificed to feed this forever-hungry Celtic Tiger. We have lost sight of the fact that as mothers and fathers we do the most important and noble work there is: we shape society from how we nurture our kids.'

It seems that the government of the day was following the debate. What happened in the 2005 budget was unexpected: a cash payment of €1000 was provided annually for every child under the age of six. This was not just an admission of the special expenses associated with a child who has not yet gone to school, but a flexible payment: the parent could decide to pass it on to a childcare provider or keep it to help him or her to stay at home.

I was asked to comment on the measure for *The Right Hook* radio programme on Newstalk and expressed my surprise and delight that the measure applied to children up to six, the official latest age for starting school. I also expressed the worry that the measure was not taxed or means-tested. I remember saying I had been given 'a suitcase of money' (with which, soon afterwards, I bought a piano). This lack of means-testing or taxation came back to haunt the next government when it hit hard times and could not afford the payment. It has proved difficult to tax it because of individualisation: how can you calculate the income of a household if the income of the members is taxed individually?

As far as kids are concerned, what usually matters is house-hold income, not how much each adult earns. The policy of individualisation, long called-for by feminists and applauded by an *Irish Times* editorial as being ahead of its time (see p. 38) made it extremely difficult for the government of 2009 to channel funds accurately to the families that most needed them. In the budget of 2009, the child benefit rate was cut by 10 per cent, although families on social welfare or receiving the family income supplement were spared.

The reason social welfare payments are *not* individualised is that it is recognised that there are cost savings when people live together. Surely, in order to recognise this, the tax liablity of an earning family should also be assessed according to its total income? Wouldn't that be more equitable? Wouldn't the regime of 'community of property', whereby both spouses would have a right to the shared income and assets of the household, by law, sort the problem of the earning spouse who will not share his or her income? Then we could tax child benefit and make it a really effective tool for equalising the chances of poorer and richer children.

In her assessment of the 2005 budget in *The Irish Times* on 27 December, Kate Holmquist made the point that the new payment was paid equally to top earners and lone parents on welfare. She also commented that it would have paid and should have paid for a year of pre-school education for pre-schoolers and it seems the succeeding government finally came around to the same view: the early childcare supplement was scrapped in April 2009 in favour of a year of free pre-school provision for all children who reached the age of between three years and three months and four years and six months before 1 September of the year in which they were to attend.

But Holmquist went on to pit 'working mothers' against 'mothers in the home':

> ...no sooner had the National Economic and Social Forum highlighted the disgraceful neglect of childcare services than the mothers-in-the-home lobby hijacked the campaign, praising themselves for their devotion to their children and, by implication, damning women who chose to combine work and family. Once the 'should mothers

work?' debate began afresh, there was no stopping it, even though it was out of touch with Irish family life in 2005.

It was obviously disempowering of working women, preying on the guilt that most working mothers seem to feel when they have difficulty coping, rather than blaming the system that makes work-life balance difficult.

The focus of the debate was stolen from where it should have been – the government's failure to provide quality, affordable childcare and was placed squarely on mothers.

Particularly disempowered were lone parents, 48 per cent of whom find themselves and their children at risk of poverty. Many young mothers are eager to get out to work so they can improve their own and their children's lives and futures.

It is OECD policy to enable lone mothers to work, breaking the poverty cycle, yet nothing was done in the budget to provide them with access to childcare.

One thing missing in the debate was sociological research into who stays home full-time and why. Many lone mothers remain in the home because they have no choice but what about married stay-at-home mothers?

What do their husbands earn, for example? Is the wife of a high-earning executive more likely to remain in the home to support her husband's status and his lifestyle and to compensate for his own work-life balance?

What are the educational qualifications of women who choose to be full-time mothers? The fact that one in five Irish mothers who are full-time in the home employ nannies and child minders didn't arise in the debate. Nobody seems too worried

that these may be the mothers for whom €1000
extra per year will mean another handbag in Brown
Thomas.

The year ended without any vision of a state-
supported childcare system in place. The people
who benefitted most were stay-at-home mothers,
who got an extra €1000 per year despite having no
childcare costs.

I agree with Kate Holmquist that the 'should mothers work?'
question is pointless and irrelevant. But I don't agree with her
that caring for children is not work. This is the implication of
the comment that at-home mothers had received the €1000 euro
early-childhood payment 'despite having no childcare costs'. The
childcare cost of an at-home mother is her foregone income.

The only way you can think of at-home mothers as having
no childcare costs is to believe they are people who never had
an income or had no need of an income. In fact, *The Irish Times/*
MRBI survey of women's behaviour and attitudes in 2007 found
that while a quarter of the women categorised by advertisers
as being in the ABC1 economic category were full-time
homemakers, 41 per cent of those in the C2DE category were
full-time home-makers (27 September 2010). Thirty-eight to 40
per cent of female homemakers are likely to have a credit or Laser
card, compared to 64 per cent of female paid workers. Nearly
twice as many female paid workers are likely to have an SSIA than
female unpaid workers. And most worryingly, only 14 per cent
of homemakers have a private or work pension compared to 42
per cent of female paid workers. Is it any wonder that full-time
homemakers so rarely appear in advertisements?

At-home mothers have no income and thanks to the policy
of individualisation, almost no tax allowance. This measure
alone could – in a worst-case scenario – leave them as much as
€7850 annually worse off than a 'working mother.' In her article
Holmquist also disregards the €500,000 which was invested
directly in childcare in the 2005 budget.

As we have seen again and again, more childcare facilities do not necessarily equal more women in the workplace. Hakim found Sweden to have the toughest glass ceiling in the industrialised world. But Sweden also has a high level of female representation in parliament: second in one hundred and thirty-seven ranked nations in 2010. It seems that in Sweden, while most women opt to stay in low-pressure jobs, those who want to get their hands on the reins of power can do so. The US, with a relatively thin glass ceiling, comes in at seventy-first in the world for female representation in parliament.

Having more women in parliament doesn't necessarily mean a more developed country: the nation with the highest number of women in parliament in the world is Rwanda. The lack of female representation in parliament is still a huge issue and serious consideration must be given as to why Ireland is coming in way down at number eighty-two in the world ranking. Increasing the numbers in itself will not give women the representation they need because these elected women will tend to be unrepresentative of the world of unpaid work. We need a political forum which includes the voice of the unpaid: parents in the home, carers, pensioners, the disabled and the unemployed.

I doubt that as many women as men will ever accept almost giving up on family life, which is the cost of being a politician in today's modern democracies. But if time rearing children were not discounted as being irrelevant to a woman's future career, perhaps more women would enter politics after a period in the home. If we were less ageist, more women who have reared their children might bring their experience to politics.

There's a theory among primatologists like Sarah Blaffer Hrdy that ascribes all of humankind's success on the planet to the fact that women often have a long life after the menopause. It was the grannies who got us where we are. Given a chance, they might think up a way of keeping us here.

# 6

# Fear and Loathing: What's our Problem with Mothers and Children?

*...the standard feminist response to the fact that child-rearing marginalises women is not to raise its status but to urge men to do more of it. Though this has been the cry for more than thirty years, almost 100 per cent of the primary caregivers of young children are still women. This suggests that feminism needs a fresh strategy.*

Ann Crittenden, *The Price of Motherhood: Why the Most Important Job in the World Is Still the Least Valued*

Yesterday was Mother's Day and I went to church with my four children. My autistic spectrum child insisted on sitting with his brother and their friends. The instinct towards sociability was positive so I let him, although I knew it could play badly. And indeed it did; very soon he got restless and argumentative. I reached my hand behind me, laid it on him and kept it there for the entire service. I'm not saying he stopped complaining but he did calm down.

No one taught me to do that. My children have given me healing hands. As the sermon reached the meaning of 'mothering' I suddenly realised that my outstretched hand said it all.

I have always disliked Mother's Day and I never celebrated it with my own mother. This no doubt dates back to a terrible event in my own childhood when I bought my mother a horrible brooch inscribed with the word 'Mother' and she said it was horrible. I still remember my father's intake of breath.

But yesterday things were different. My daughter arrived

downstairs, purple with pride, and produced a homemade card from behind her back which read 'Happy Mumer's Day.' It was my turn to turn purple with pride.

I don't know why I'm so interested in children. I had, after all, a mother who told me often – when I was a child – that she didn't like children. This may well be at the heart of it; I still feel the outrage of a child at that comment. And my father, although busy and distant, always treated me like a full human being. He would ask my advice.

I had in my parents an unusual combination of a father who built my sense of my own importance and a mother who did not. This is probably the rocket fuel in my concern for children's rights.

There is an incredible, out-of-print book by Joseph Robins called *A Study of Charity Children in Ireland 1700-1900*. I have read it several times. There is something in me that responds to the horror stories of how children were treated, as if I'm being awakened to a suppressed memory. I think children have a genetic memory of their mistreatment – or possibly just a clear sense of their vulnerability and of what this could mean for their chances of survival in another kind of society, the kind of society that is in the recent past in this part of the world and in the present in many others.

It is, in evolutionary terms, only the blink of an eye since 1737 when the bodies of thirteen 'branded' infants were found in a sandpit. Their wet nurses had received an 'advance' for feeding them but had done away with them or left them to die. The brands the babies had on their arms were a new measure to stop the wet nurses substituting other children, including their own, for the ones they were meant to be feeding. Retrospective payments didn't work either – another trick wet nurses had was to soak the bodies of dead babies in water to increase their weight so that they could claim payment for having fed for longer than they did.

Many infants died even before they arrived at the Dublin Foundling Hospital. They often had their clothes stolen on the journey. Even if they arrived alive, they were unlikely to survive.

The gate porter who accepted the children and gave a receipt for them also had the duty of disposing of their bodies if they died:

> For the sake of convenience burials were confined to three days a week. Between burial days, the dead infants accumulated and the porter, in evidence, stated that he had buried as many as thirteen at one time. Wrapped in grey blankets, the bodies were taken to a field at the back of the hospital and interred there. So frequent were the burials that the field was completely bare of grass. A sub-committee set up to inspect the conditions in the hospital lamented the necessity of having to report facts 'which carry a complexion of more than savage cruelty'.

The idea of a child as a full human being with rights is recent. Jesus Christ got it – 'Theirs is the Kingdom of Heaven' – but two thousand years later most of us are still catching up. It has become clear to me while writing this book that children's rights are the women's rights of today. Theirs is the area of rights which is in sudden and dramatic evolution. Just as our concept of womanhood exploded thirty or forty years ago, so today our concept of childhood is exploding.

Just as with women's rights, our understanding of children's rights has been a dawning realisation. The UN Convention on the Rights of the Child has its roots in Eglantyne Jebb's Declaration of the Rights of the Child adopted by the League of Nations in 1924 but not adopted by the UN General Assembly until 1989. Ireland ratified it in 1992. Of the nations of the world, one hundred and ninety-three have ratified, leaving just the US and Somalia in the doghouse.

The wide-ranging convention establishes human rights for children on a par with those of adults but understands them as needing 'special care and assistance'. Where possible, it says, they should be brought up in a family, by their own parents. The 'best

interests of the child' must be 'a primary consideration' in 'all
actions concerning children, whether undertaken by public or
private social welfare institutions, courts of law, administrative
authorities or legislative bodies...' The convention is a bar which
the nations of the world have been trying to clear ever since. In
2006 Ireland was still being criticised by the UN Committee on
the Rights of the Child for having failed fully to incorporate the
convention into domestic law. But in truth there has been a sea-
change in the importance given to children's rights since Ireland's
agreement to ratify in 1992.

The turn of the millennium may have been a damp squib in
many ways but it marked an explosion in the recognition of
children in Irish society. The *National Children's Strategy* was
published in 2000, again enshrining the 'welfare principle' in
policy affecting children and stating that 'the best interests of the
child should be the primary concern of decision-making'. The
strategy included strong measures including the establishment of
a Dáil na nÓg (children's parliament) run jointly by the Minister
for Children and the National Youth Council of Ireland; the
appointment of an Ombudsman for Children; the establishment
of the National Children's Office and the National Children's
Advisory Council; the establishment of the National Children's
Research Dissemination Unit and then a National Longitudinal
Study of Children. The appointment of Brian Lenihan as the first
full cabinet minister for children in 2005 was a central piece in the
tapestry.

In 2010 an Oireachtas committee came up with new wording
to amend the Constitution to strengthen children's rights in line
with the UN Convention and it is to be hoped that a referendum
will be held in the near future.

Applying some detachment, it is possible to see these
measures in their historical context of exponential economic
growth. It seems beyond doubt that nothing diminishes children's
rights like poverty. The economic ability to raise children well is a
good first step to making us want to do it. Having fewer children
tends to give us a better chance of raising well the ones we have.

It was inevitable that more concern for children's rights would follow economic wellbeing in Ireland.

Our vision of what a childhood should be is shaped, to some extent, by what we can afford. Until the era of compulsory schooling, not much more than a century ago in many parts of the world, children were important members of the workforce. As Colin Heywood records in *A History of Childhood* (2001), the earliest spinning machinery of the late eighteenth century was designed to be used by children to reduce labour costs; the first spinning mill using the machinery in the United States employed a hundred children between four and ten. Compulsory schooling, when enforced, ushered in the era in which the child became 'economically useless but emotionally priceless'.

But it may be that our current huge investment in children has an economic root as well. Compulsory schooling developed when economies needed highly educated – and intensively parented – workers. Ann Crittenden argues that the kind of rearing with which a modern mother tries to provide her child developed as a result of economic possibilities and pressures. She notes that numerous foreign travellers to the US in the early nineteenth century remarked how young mothers were swallowed up by the job of rearing their children and explains:

> The increasing weight given to the job of caring for children was far more than just a strategy to distract women from participating in public life. It was also necessary to the development of a vibrant, capitalist economy. By the late eighteenth century in France, England, and the United states, the countries with the most dynamic economies of the day, understood that their children would have to become educated little achievers if they were going to improve or even maintain their station in life. This required a new approach to child-rearing.'

Because industrialisation distanced men from the home, women had to take up the task of home-educator almost on their own. Hence, according to Crittenden, began the drive to educate women: so that they could mother educated workers.

This part of the story is never told: what is told is that most industrial activity had left the home by the mid-nineteenth century. What really happened was that the kind of work done at home changed: women were, as Crittenden writes, 'recruited to the crucial task of producing the kind of human capital that the modern industrial society needed'.

It stands to reason that in Ireland, where industrialisation was delayed and in many areas never happened, the development of intensive rearing was delayed too. In fact, our 'stay-at-home' mothers of the past were more likely to be busy farmers' wives than dedicated home-educators. My mother, who had me late in life and would be ninety this year, grew up on a farm in County Donegal but her parents were both teachers who valued education hugely. I don't know if they valued home-education, though, and I don't believe my mother felt she had a role as my educator.

It's possible that the whole trip about the importance of child-rearing hit some Irish families for the first time in the person of mothers now raising children. It's also possible that the whole trip about the importance of their own education to the workplace hit the same families for the first time in the person of these same mothers. Because of our jagged graph of economic and social development since independence, the same pressures that pit-patted down on women throughout the developed world have, I think, hailed down on Irish women of my generation.

The most informed comparison I can make is with the UK, because I am tuned into UK media every day. I find that in Britain the debate about mothers and children has moved on from reactionary feminism to a much greater extent than it has in Ireland. My favourite example of this contrast so far was the presentation of one of Lucy Kellaway's *Financial Times* columns, syndicated in *The Irish Times* on 9 February 2009. With self-deprecating humour, Kellaway wrote that she had been pushed by a report called, *A Good Childhood: Searching for Values in a Competitive Age*, published by the Children's Society, to wonder for the first time if her focus on her career verged, at times, on the selfish.

The headline on the piece in *The Irish Times* was 'Can you be ambitious for yourself and your children?' and the highlighted quotation was 'I am not planning to stop working and start baking cakes.' This was such a misrepresentation of the thrust of the article that I looked up the headline in its original form in *The Financial Times*. It ran, "My new guilt as a selfish working mother" and the highlighted quotation was 'Life remains a succession of uneasy compromises, but this report on childhood has changed the way I think.'

Women of my generation have become mothers at a time when the economy demanded women both as workers and as child-rearers and the two demands were frequently on a collision course. There is, in truth, a tension between the perceived rights of women and the perceived needs of children. The two 'rights' revolutions, those of women and those of children, are often in open conflict.

Every effort is made to pretend that this is not so, with the result that elements of children's needs are often officially denied. Even some of the progressive measures for children introduced in this country have to be examined in case they are really about getting mothers into the workplace.

The *National Children's Strategy* (2000) records that the 'recent development of a constricted labour supply has implications for the economic wellbeing of the country'. What possible place has this statement in a strategy for the wellbeing of children? Well, you can argue that the country can't produce enough wealth for the children if the women aren't working. But you can argue back that there are different kinds of wealth and, indeed, different kinds of poverty.

Just because *The National Children's Strategy* reports on the 'benefits of early childhood programmes' for children, don't whip your children out of the kitchen to the nearest pre-school. The strategy takes its information from the Expert Working Group on Childcare's *National Childcare Strategy* (1999), which namechecks Schweinhart and Weikart, who in turn take their information from the Perry Pre-school Project which was set up in the US in the early 1960s and *which reported exclusively on children born in poverty.*

Remember that the childcare strategy was specifically addressing the needs of women in the workforce, women whose children are usually *not* among the most disadvantaged in our community.

It is clear that children from disadvantaged homes benefit enormously from pre-school programmes. The less your home offers you, the more you will benefit from pre-school. The more your home offers you, the less you will benefit from pre-school. The National Economic and Social Forum's *Early Childhood and Education* document (2005) clearly states that the benefits of pre-school to advantaged children will be 'less (if any)' than for disadvantaged children because their home life is 'closer to the quality of childcare they receive in pre-school'.

I'm not saying that children from advantaged homes shouldn't go to pre-school. It may do them some good and is unlikely to do them any harm. It might mean a child with special needs will be diagnosed earlier. And there's hardly a parent who won't appreciate a few hours' grace. But the strongest reason for advantaged children to go to pre-school is that their presence will provide disadvantaged children with a much better environment than they would have without them.

The idea gaining ground that you cannot raise your pre-school child at home because you do not have the expertise is ideologically-driven. It relates to our boom-time economic need to professionalise child rearing so that well-educated women can stay at work. From the point of view of growth-motivated economists, it was all about more 'productivity'. For some women's organisations it's been about getting women into jobs because that's what's good for them.

This means denying totally the need for any skill on the part of the parent. At times it goes as far as to imply that parents have no skills for educating pre-school children. But Fergus Finlay, director of children's charity Barnardos, says what he needs most of all are 'skilled mothers. Effective mothers.'

He goes so far as to say:

> We don't want to work with a child without working with a mum. All of our work is aimed at supporting mums. There's nothing more fundamental in terms of this country's future than motherhood. Ninety per cent of the problems kids face are parenting-related. These parents love their kids and don't know how to be effective parents. Ninety per cent of the mothers we know don't know how to say, 'No,' to their kids. There's a lack of confidence and a lack of skill. No boundaries were ever introduced.

He paints a picture of families in which children get up when they want, go to school if they want, eat what they want.

'The most important thing in a child's life is the love of a mother,' says Finlay. 'The less pressure there is on her and the less stress and strain, the better. If we really want the future to be better for all of us we need to discharge the debt we have to motherhood. We need to help mothers to be the best they can be.'

I tell him that some would say this kind of talk gets in the way of women's success in work outside the home. 'Everybody has to strike their own balance,' he says. 'If career matters, it matters.'

As to the argument made by many quoted already in this book that parenting is a waste of a woman's education, Finlay says it's 'nonsense': 'The link between mother's education and that of the kids is crystal-clear. Children whose mothers don't have education start secondary school two years behind those whose mothers are educated.' The disadvantage continues right through the educational cycle.

Nor does this mean that it is a waste for an educated woman

to work *outside* the home. It just means that all those hours we educated mothers spend helping with homework really matter, as do, of course, all the other gifts our education has brought us.

It is very interesting that this work of motherhood is under-valued. Motherhood is never seen as active, skilful or effective. It is in the absence of any sense of the value of the work of mother-hood that recommendations can be made that exactly equal amounts should be done by male and female partners, regardless of the skills they have. It is in fact vitally important that the best skills on offer to a child should the best available in the family: in crude terms, if Mammy can read and Daddy can't, Mammy should supervise the homework.

I know a couple in which the husband is currently un-employed and the wife is working part-time in a very well-paid job. She could go full-time but she doesn't want to because she is a very skilled teacher, her children are young and one has a learning disability. They're just going to try to hold out until Dad gets another job. Mum is too valuable at home to be full-time in the workplace.

The Nobel Prize-winning economist Gary Becker has analysed family life from an economic perspective and sees specialisation of tasks as a simple matter of efficiency. Just as in business, certain people in families will specialise in performing certain tasks. The reason women are nearly always the childcare specialists in any family is because, he writes, they tend to have slightly better childcare skills. The women invest so much in the gestation, birth and nursing of their children that they tend to want to rear them and make sure the investment pays off.

Cultural images of motherhood are nearly always passive, whereas the reality of motherhood – including birth, if you get the chance – is active in the extreme. You end up fighting fascism when you fight for mothers: a *Kinder, Kuche, Kirche* version of motherhood which is passive and imposed from outside. I think Irishwomen are remaking motherhood as active and liberated with enormous speed and this is contributing to our high birth rate. But there is still evident in 'official' Ireland – the media, government and government-funded women's advocacy groups – a strong reaction to the perception that a passive motherhood role was envisaged by de Valera's Ireland. Article 41.2 of the 1937 constitution is quoted again and again to show definitively that Irishwomen are downtrodden. The wording is: 'In particular the state recognises that by her life within the home, woman gives to the state a support without which the common good cannot be achieved. The state shall, therefore, endeavour to ensure that mothers shall not be obliged by economic necessity to engage in labour to the neglect of their duties in the home.'

Historian Caitriona Clear writes in *Women of the House* that this article 'is often believed to have contributed, more than anything else, to women's inequality in twentieth-century Ireland'. But she adds: 'De Valera's irritation at feminist opposition to the constitution suggests that he did not inhabit a political environment that was entirely indifferent to women's views: indeed, he told the late Professor T.P. O'Neill that Ivy Pinchbeck's *Women Workers and the Industrial Revolution* (1933) had a major impact on his thinking and forced his attention onto protecting Irish women and children from the worst effects of what he hoped was Ireland's industrial revolution.'

It seems that the idea, which I had myself for some time, that Article 41.2 was aimed at immuring women in their homes, is simplistic. But it is equally clear that the Article is of its time and should be removed or changed. There was an aspiration in the programme for government agreed in 2009 by the Green Party and Fianna Fáil, that there should be a referendum to amend the constitution to refer to the 'parent in the home'. This would be welcome. I don't think, however, that such play would need to be made of the equal care responsibilities of men and women if caring were valued. It's because it's undervalued that there's an emphasis on splitting it. Can you imagine a stipulation in the constitution that women and men should have equal earning responsibilities? There would be no necessity for it because, although going out and earning money is very often not all it's cracked up to be, it is currently the socially acceptable thing to do. But positive constitutional recognition of the work of caring, which is irreplaceable yet does not feature in any calculation of GNP or pay-related benefits, would be a start.

Understanding that the most important education inter-ventions in children's early years are the interventions that luckier parents can provide themselves means understanding just how much skilled work most parents do. Looking at the room for the very young participants in Barnardos' early education programme in Loughlinstown, County Dublin, I was struck by the toy kitchen, a staple of all good pre-school environments: a little cooker, little drawers, little pots and pans. Kerry Smith, Assistant Director of Barnardos in Dublin South, agrees straight away that banging around a *real* kitchen at home in the attentive presence of a parent will do the job just as well – but the attentive presence of a parent is not an advantage every child has. Some parents, she says, don't know how to play with their children, often because they were never played with as children.

Economic disadvantage seems to be the background of most of the children referred to the centre, with all the different types of dysfunction that can come with such disadvantage. The Barnardos centres are genuinely child-centred childcare centres but Smith feels that most childcare services are built around 'the needs of industry, not children and families'. Pre-school children come to the Loughlinstown centre four mornings a week. Smith would not advocate long hours of centre-based care for small children. 'There's this misconception that group care is safer than care with a single minder,' she says. 'But two to three hours a day, or maybe four, that's the maximum they should be in group care.'

Penelope Leach makes a fascinating point about crèches in *Children First*, which has spent more than a decade lodged at the back of my mind. She says their 'relative impersonality may be more important to some parents than they themselves realise'; they feel less guilty than they would leaving their child with a child minder who is just like them except she is with the child all day, while they are not; and also less fearful that the child will have a minder whose bond with him challenges his bond with his parents. Indeed, I remember one of my friends telling me that she deliberately chose a crèche for her baby because she didn't want the sole influence of another woman on her child.

Babies and small children respond to individuals, not to a business model, and they can't put that responsiveness on ice for the working day. Best practice in crèches is to put in place measures which mimic a good family set-up, like appointing a 'key worker' to interact with each child and liaise with his or her parents. The attachment between their child and another adult that some parents fear is actually necessary to their development.

Barbara Gavagan appoints 'key workers' for the children in the bright, purpose-built Fatima Mansions Day Care Centre in Dublin, which Fergus Finlay described to me as an example of 'best practice'. She doesn't take babies until they are a year old because, she says, babies need 'the nurture of a family'. Her service runs from 9am to 5pm and, although those hours don't cover a working day and a commute. She says, 'We don't feel that 8am to 6pm is an appropriate amount of time for children to spend in anyone else's care other than their parents.'

Again, economic disadvantage is the background of many children in the area. Some of the children who come to the centre would be in full-time care if it weren't for the intervention of the day care centre, which allows them to stay in their families. Part-time hours are offered as a matter of course. Barbara Gavagan herself, whose own child is in the centre full-time, says she would opt for her child to go part-time if a family member could stay at home.

The bulk of our childcare was not designed with the child as its focus. The first major drive to provide childcare places in Ireland was the Equal Opportunities Childcare Programme (2000-2006) supported by the EU to get women into the workplace. It was administered by the Department of Justice, Equality and Law Reform, which, as Gavagan says, has 'nothing remotely got to do with children'. Funded to the tune of €500 million, its aim of creating 31,800 childcare places was exceeded. This was succeeded by the *National Childcare Strategy 2006-2010* which was funded by the state to the tune of €575 million, €358 of which was to be capital investment. It aimed to create another 50,000 childcare places, including 5000 after-school places and 10,000 pre-school places.

This massive increase in the number of childcare places was allowed without any regulations about the level of training required by each member of staff or the provision of a key worker to every child or the number of hours the children should spend in care. Under the Childcare Act, 1991, any service caring for more than three pre-school children has to notify the Health Service Executive, which will at some point check your facility. But what they're checking are the health and safety standards, not the educational standards. They're checking the facility, not the children. Two new documents on training and curriculum, *Síolta* and *Aistear*, were developed by now closed Centre for Early Childhood Development and Education at St Patrick's College, Drumcondra, but their use is not mandatory and they are not even widely understood.

It's all been about creating as many places as possible in as short a time as possible so that as many women as possible could get out and work. The terms of reference of the National Childcare Strategy (2000) were specifically working parents, as Professor Nóirín Hayes, expert in early education, reminded me in a recent interview: 'Without any vision for children that was agreed we got a structure which is not sitting comfortably with the Irish people, centre-based care which a lot of people don't want.'

What do they want? They favour child-minding and family day-care, she says. 'Lots of Irish families want their children together. They don't want their babies here and their toddlers there.' She mentions a model of childcare in Portugal in which a net of child minders is supported by a centre:

> People will look back at the Equal Opportunities Childcare Programme and the National Childcare Programme and they'll say it was successful because

the number of places was created and the children
filled them. But actually 54 per cent of the EOCP,
particularly, went to the construction industry.
And even if the other 50 per cent went to training
and quality...But no, it went to the setting up of
structures: the thirty-three city and county childcare
committees, the national childcare coordinator,
investing in the national voluntary organisations
because we let them do the work.

What will people think of all this when they look back?
'They're going to be appalled,' she says.

Particularly worrying are the planning guidelines of June 2001
which aimed to multiply the number of childcare places through
the mechanism of forcing builders to provide one childcare
service for every seventy-five houses built. This seems to have
been a particularly rough cocktail of providing support to the
building industry and women for the workplace.

'Access to quality childcare services contributes to the social,
emotional and educational development of children,' announce
the guidelines, without specifying, of course, which children and
which childcare services. Having got that bit over, the guidelines
continue: 'There are clear economic benefits from the provision
of childcare. The lack of accessible, affordable and appropriate
childcare facilities makes it difficult for many parents/guardians
to access employment and employment-related opportunities.
Childcare is also a potential area of employment in its own right
and needs to be supported to ensure it can achieve its potential in
this regard.'

The places are to be created in:

the vicinity of concentrations of workplaces, such
as industrial estates, business parks and any other
locations where there are significant numbers
working. The site, location and layout of facilities
should optimise the opportunities for safe and

efficient journeys to and from the workplace of parents/guardians. This may be achieved by locating the facility close to the entrance to the business park/ industrial estate so that all parents/guardians would automatically pass it on their way to work and would not have to detour past their workplace in order to drop off children.

No information seems to have been gathered as to how well this policy is working nationally but a brief trawl through the property websites reveals that many of these purpose-built crèches are now on the market. In Meath, a county over-developed as a dormitory for Dublin, prospective owners are encouraged to buy a crèche which would have a better turnover 'if the regulations in relation to ratio of children to space are relaxed or if the mix of full-time to part-time children was adjusted in favour of more full-time children.'

Where is the UN Convention's 'welfare principle' in all of this? How can we possibly argue that 'the best interests of the child' have been 'a primary consideration' in this development? How can we argue that 'the best interests of the child' have been '*the* primary concern of decision-making' as the National Children's Strategy says they should be?

We can't. We were following an economic model in which there was little place for children and, by extension, for mothers.

'There's never been a doubt in my mind that the role of women in Ireland has always been to service something subsidiary to the workforce,' says Fergus Finlay. 'When they had to give up their jobs under the marriage bar it was so that the men could have the jobs. Then we had Budget 1999 and tax individualisation whose primary objective was to drive women into the workforce.' It was, he says, 'the most socially regressive measure taken in my lifetime, without any properly thought-out approach to childcare or childhood allowances.' He adds, 'The whole debate around childcare has always been about the needs of the economy and has never had anything to do with children. Never.'

Do we in Ireland have a particular dislike for children?

Our recent history would seem to suggest so. Maybe the extent to which children were abused in Ireland was no greater than elsewhere but we specialised in institutional abuse because we specialised in institutionalisation. Long after the UK had abandoned the institutional care of orphans we were still putting them in orphanages and industrial schools.

Why did we have such confidence in institutions? Have we some terrible fear of the influence of the mother?

We were also out on our own in our willingness to institution-alise mothers. Asylums for 'fallen' women were not an Irish or Catholic idea and were originally meant to 'rehabilitate' prostitutes but in Ireland they became the prison-like Magdalen laundries where women considered deviant in any way were incarcerated, often for life. Long after the practice had been abandoned elsewhere, Ireland's laundries continued: the last one did not close until 1996. The 'penitents' frequently suffered emotional and physical abuse from the nuns in charge of them, whom, by a horrible irony, they were sometimes encouraged to address as 'Mother'.

Why did we need to shut these women away? It seems as if we feared the potentially destabilising force of their sexuality, of which children were proof?

Do we fear children because we fear sex? Do we fear children because we fear mothers?

Nóirín Hayes draws my attention to the famous débâcle of the Mother and Child Scheme in 1951. The Minister for Health, Noel Browne, campaigned for an extended care scheme for mothers and children, highlighting the fact that our infant mortality rate was twice that of the UK and that the death rate of babies under one year was similar to the death rate from TB. He resigned from the Fine Gael-led coalition government because it did not back his proposed new health service for mothers and children against the Catholic bishops, who feared a dilution of the Church's authority in sexual matters. Hayes sees it as an example of 'that sort of cruel notion that too much charity isn't a good thing'. She brings it all back to the 'traditional Catholic' construction of 'the Virgin Mother and the Mammy': 'We are a Christian country and way down deep in what we are, we view children as trouble.'

Thomas Walsh, an educational historian and development officer at the Centre of Childhood Development and Education, St Patrick's College, Drumcondra, argued in a paper at the *Voice and Images of Childhood and Adolescence* conference in Dublin in 2004 that while the needs of the economy dominated other educational systems, the perceived need for moral guidance dominated ours. We were obsessed with original sin. We were also obsessed, in our educational system, with nation-building. And we spatchcocked our notions of purity on to our notions of nation.

To echo Fergus Finlay, the debate has never been about children. Never.

But I won't swallow the idea put about by some that it's all the fault of the Catholic Church. As a 'non-Catholic' in a country with a Catholic majority, I have the luxury of detachment, which makes me either objective or ignorant, depending on your opinion. I watched in disbelief the anti-Catholic hysteria that emerged after shocking revelations of child sex abuse in Catholic institutions were published in reports of the Commission to Enquire into Child Abuse. Irish people genuinely seemed to believe that it was only in Catholic institutions that child abuse happens, whereas the truth is that abuse can happen in any institutional setting but is far more likely to happen in families.

Norman Ruddock, a Church of Ireland priest, wrote in his memoir, *The Rambling Rector* (2005), that he was abused as a young boy and later in a Church of Ireland college which he described as 'a citadel of repressive sexuality and abuse'. In the course of my own middle-class Protestant childhood I was aware of two peers who were abused in an educational setting.

As I was finishing this book in the summer and autumn of 2010, the news broke of two hundred and nineteen unmarked graves in Mount Jerome Cemetery, Harold's Cross, which were those of children who died in the Protestant Bethany Home in

Rathgar. The causes of death included heart failure, convulsions and malnutrition and the children died in their droves: there were forty deaths between 1935 and 1936. It is pretty clear, in short, that they died because of neglect of a similar character to the neglect recorded in the Dublin Foundling Hospital in the 1700s (see pp. 96-7)

The Bethany Home closed in 1972 and I must have been driven past it many times as a young child on my way to see my Auntie May. But I doubt if I would have then seen anything strange in the fact that some Irish children had such a terrible start in life by comparison with mine. I remember the condescension with which I viewed the 'orphans' who crossed my path, and how I secretly scorned their poor health and poor clothes.

Our fear of poverty has surely always been the main force behind our fear of children. As a people, we went into a kind of voluntary liquidation in the early twentieth century. By the 1950s, a quarter of the Irish did not marry at all, as opposed to only one tenth of the British, and Father John O'Brien wrote, in a famous pamphlet about the phenomenon called *The Vanishing Irish*: 'The Irish nation is slowly but surely vanishing from the fact of the earth.'

When I was growing up, the sexual repression of lonely spinsters and bachelors waiting to inherit the family farm was the stock-in-trade of plays and short stories. Their reluctance to marry was often attributed to the Catholic Church's emphasis on celibacy but wasn't it more likely that the Catholic Church was providing a rationale for a strategy to avoid poverty?

This argument is strengthened by the fact that Irish Protestants seemed to have the same problems, as Mary Kenny writes in *Goodbye to Catholic Ireland*.

She argues that the underlying reasons for the rate of celibacy were economic:

> ...without hopes for improving economic circumstances, sensible people do not marry and

beget families. And since the horrors of the 1845
Famine, Irish people had been very sensible indeed
about not founding new families where they did not
have the means to do so.

It is interesting to see that this pattern re-emerged in my
generation during the recession of the 1980s, as sociologist
Mary Corcoran showed in her memorable study of émigrés to
the US, *Irish Illegals: Transients between Two Societies*. When we
left the country, not only did we often fail to marry abroad, we
often failed to form relationships. Although we had the option
of contraception, we often stayed celibate and waited for that
sometimes mythical return to Ireland to 'settle down'.

I think the Irish have tended to explain away an avoidance of
children for economic reasons by blaming it on the emphasis on
celibacy in Catholic doctrine. I'm not saying that there is not an
inherent fear of children and mothers in some interpretations
of the Catholic tradition. It is interesting that Colin Heywood
can speak of distinctly Catholic and Protestant ways of dealing
with unwanted children from the eighteenth century to the
early twentieth century. This trend has shown some evidence of
continuing. Italy passed legislation to close her orphanages in
2001; foster care was still unusual there at that time. The countries
best known for their orphanages in recent years have been the
countries of the former Communist block, which were secular,
but had mostly been Orthodox.

Why? Did the Catholic or Orthodox emphasis on the
institution rather than the individual inform policy on children?
Did the perceived need to save a child's soul come before the need
to save his or her sanity?

I don't know. But if the Irish fear of mothers and hatred of
children were all the fault of Catholicism, one would expect other
Catholic societies to show similar patterns. And they don't. Italy
was poor, Catholic and exporting her people by the boatload in
the 1950s but her fertility rate, at 2.3 children per adult woman,
was still above replacement level. It is now that Italy is 'vanishing'

– with a birth rate of 1.3 children per adult woman in 2010 – because of its economic and political paralysis.

It's easy to point the finger at Catholicism and, indeed, the Christian tradition in general, when trying to explain our Irish unease with mothers and children. No one is going to disagree with you. No one you know, anyway, if you work in the media in Ireland. Your problems start when, like me, you point the finger at our growth-obsessed economy and when you see, in the feminist tradition which has not questioned it, echoes of that very same unease with mothers and children.

What seems clear to me now is what is only logical: our feminist tradition did not represent a clean break with the other forces which have shaped us, including poverty and a version of Catholicism designed to control it. Instead, our feminism and our feminists were shaped by these forces. And went on to shape me.

# 7

# Birth Pains: Ireland's Birth Industry

*'Don't do a hysterectomy on me.'*
Valerie Neary's words to Dr Michael Neary
after the birth of her child, as told to the Fitness
to Practice Committee of the Medical Council

The Neary nightmare seems to dramatise the fear of motherhood that is one of the themes of this book. Between 1974 and 1998 Dr Michael Neary of Our Lady of Lourdes Hospital, Drogheda, removed the wombs of 129 women who had just had babies. In the period between 1992 and 1998 his rate of 'peripartum hysterectomy' as these procedures are called, was twenty times that recorded in the National Maternity Hospital, Dublin.

Most of these operations were probably unnecessary. We can never know exactly how many, because the files of more than forty of the women are missing. They were systematically stolen from the hospital once suspicions were raised. In some ways this crime is worse than the crime of the unnecessary hysterectomies, because although it is possible that Dr Neary did not deliberately do harm, the thief deliberately stole from women their right to truth.

It is the spectre of the woman who begged Dr Neary not to take her womb that haunts me most. She was not out cold like many of Neary's victims, some of whom didn't know their wombs were missing until weeks later. No, she had had an epidural and was awake. And she reason she knew exactly what was happening was because she was a midwife at the Our Lady of Lourdes Hospital.

Valerie Neary (no relation) was five days overdue with her second baby in August 1996. She went into labour but told the Fitness to Practice Committee of the Medical Council that she had made 'little progress' overnight and had asked for an epidural. Dr Neary suggested an oxytocin drip to speed up the labour but by morning she was not ready to deliver. Dr Neary suggested a C-section and she consented. Going into the operating theatre she asked her husband to make sure her womb wasn't taken.

Her baby was born. But then the nightmare began. Dr Neary said she was bleeding heavily. Valerie told the Fitness to Practice Committee, as retold in Sheila O'Connor's book on the consultant, *Without Consent* (2010):

'I had realised there were a lot of hysterectomies being carried out at the hospital over the previous year and was beginning to panic. He turned around a couple of minutes later and said, "I have to carry out a hysterectomy."

'One of the midwives was crying. She was looking down with tears in her eyes.

'A ward sister came in through the theatre doors. "Dr Neary, we will get Dr Lynch in," she said.'

Dr Neary called for his hysterectomy instruments and cut out her womb. The midwives present remember him saying there was a defect in her womb because of a drug her mother had taken to stop her milk coming when she had Valerie. This was a reason he commonly gave for the incidence of defective wombs but there does not seem to be a scientific basis for it. Two years later, Valerie Neary asked for her pathology notes and found out there was nothing wrong with her womb. Dr Neary was found guilty of professional misconduct in her case.

It's the most shocking scene in the Saffron Films-RTÉ docudrama *Whistleblower* screened in 2009 and I watched it from the corner of the couch, chewing a cushion. All Neary's needless operations were appalling in their own way but the sight of a professional midwife begging for her womb, watched by another midwife and a nurse and then being mutilated in front of them, will stay with me for life. It's the women's awful helplessness in the face of institutional power that affected me most. Valerie Neary lost her womb because of a strict hierarchy in which men ruled and women served.

Judge Maureen Harding Clark, who conducted the Lourdes Hospital Enquiry which reported in 2006, buys into the idea that Neary had a pathological fear of blood: colleagues talk of him sweating 'profusely' when he saw heavy bleeding. A colleague describes him in a chilling phrase as a 'dry worker'. She also says that he had a personality defect which meant he could not appreciate the impact of the loss of her womb to a woman – even when those women were in their teens or twenties and were starting their families. Even the women whose babies died and who are now childless.

One victim had her womb removed after the birth of her first baby at nineteen. She didn't find out until more than a week later when Neary tipped her on the toes, said, 'No more babies for you', and walked away. Her files are missing. Another discovered her womb was gone only when she breast-fed her baby and did not feel it 'cringe'.

Maybe Neary just didn't like women's reproductive organs. They can cause you trouble, after all, and you can live without them. So why not just get rid of them?

It wasn't just wombs that Neary took out, it was ovaries. More than forty women have so far been judged deserving of compensation for the wrongful removal of their ovaries. Some were told they had endometriosis which might develop into cancer. Mostly they didn't have it at all and in any case it can't develop into cancer. Some had benign cysts requiring limited surgery but Neary took out their ovaries. This not only made them infertile but plunged them into a horribly early menopause.

One case, described by Harding Clark as 'surprising', involved a woman in her thirties who attended Dr Neary with what she thought was a gynaecological problem but may have been a miscarriage. Neary booked her in for a routine diagnostic D and C (emptying of the womb's contents) but instead took out her womb, ovaries and fallopian tubes. Apparently, he believed she had cancer but he never mentioned this to her and in any case she didn't. Why didn't he stop the operation when he saw no evidence of the disease?

The fear of blood was obviously not the issue in these cases. Richard Porter and Roger Clements, who conducted a 2007 enquiry into the cases of the women whose ovaries were removed, raise the question of Neary's intentions:

> Dr Neary appears to have reached diagnoses, frequently incorrectly, based on clinical examination alone and on that basis performed radical surgery, even though at operation it was clear that the diagnosis had been incorrect. Yet faced with the facts at the time of surgery he continued in very many cases to deprive women of their reproductive organs and their own sex hormones. In our view the recurrent nature of this behaviour, and the absence of evidence of inadequate surgical technique, raises very troubling questions about his motives.

Harding Clark says it is important to remember that this is a case in which 'nobody died'; but people were deprived of life, the unborn babies Neary's victims never had. Their great grief is the tragic expression of something this society has found hard to admit: women's longing for children of their own. Although the Neary case is extreme, the hard reality is that it is in many ways symptomatic of the way the Irish birth industry is structured, which is in turn symptomatic of how Irish society is structured.

Harding Clark's enquiry into peripartum hysterectomy at Our Lady of Lourdes Hospital sketches the history very well. The Medical Missionaries of Mary founded the hospital in 1939. It was founded with a 'missionary zeal' in an era of hardship which had medical staff struggling with primitive conditions – such as no hot water. The nuns may have been 'of unusually strong character' but convent life made them used to hierarchies and they said it was part of their training as nurses not to question authority. A culture of silent obedience prevailed.

There are wider issues relating to the Irish health system which allowed the Neary scandal to happen. The Our Lady of Lourdes began its life as a private hospital The North-Eastern Health Board bought it in 1997; at one point there was the, in hindsight, terrifying prospect that Dr Neary himself would bid for it, along with another consultant.

Another issue is the over-medicalisation of childbirth in this country, which is linked to the power of consultants. In Valerie Neary's case, for instance, we need to look not just at the removal of her womb but at the interventions which led up to it: the epidural injection into her spine, which deadened her body from the waist and slowed her labour down; the oxytocin drip, designed to speed her labour up. She may have needed none of these interventions.

The Caesarean rate at Our Lady of Lourdes was high, as was the rate of induction of labour with oxytocin, both of which were noted by the Institute of Obstetricians Review Group in 1999. If the Caesarean rate had been lower, so would the number of women who had their wombs amputated for no reason.

Increased blood loss and hysterectomy are among the known risks of Caesarean section. Others include infection, respiratory complications from anaesthesia and reactions to anaesthesia. The risk of maternal death is four times higher during Caesarean section than during vaginal birth. The risks to the baby include respiratory problems and injury during surgery.

In Ireland, the national rate of Caesarean section is about 25 per cent while the World Health Organisation recommends a rate of 15 per cent. We also have high levels of all the other interventions, which in their turn can lead to more interventions: oxytocin drips, epidurals, instrumental delivery. Although I was told repeatedly in the course of this research that Ireland had the lowest level of infant mortality in the world – and it is low – 2008 statistics show that ten European countries and Japan have lower rates than we do.

Who are you under?' asked my boss in *The Irish Times* when I told him I was pregnant. I replied, rather curtly, that I was on top.

My mother wanted to pay for me to go to some 'big name' obstetrician. She was very worried by my decision to go semi-private in the National Maternity Hospital. I don't know why it mattered so much to her who I was 'under', considering that her own experience of birth consisted of having her face slathered with Vaseline and being knocked out cold with ether. When you woke up, apparently, your baby was washed, dressed and in its cot. She often told me about this but also about the public patient labouring beside her without the 'benefit' of ether, who was being treated with ignorance and rudeness by the nurses: 'Come on, Mrs Healy!' My mother protested about the treatment the woman was getting and was told, 'Ah, her – she'll be back in again next year with another.'

My husband's great-grandmother was a midwife in west Cork in the early part of the twentieth century. I imagine her cycling off on country roads to attend mothers at dead of night. Of course birth is not always romantic and the rates of maternal and infant death during that era were very high by today's standards. But many social factors have contributed to a radical improvement in those figures, not just the Comhairle na nOspidéal recommendation in 1976 that all births should take place in consultant-led hospitals.

This finished the process of taking control of birth away from women. We have, for the most part, care in childbirth led by powerful male consultants. Individually, they often give women superb care. Collectively, they stick together to protect one another and maintain power. This was most clearly seen in the 1998 peer review of Neary's Caesarean hysterectomies between 1996 and 1998, conducted by three obstetricians from Dublin teaching hospitals. They concluded that 'the mothers of the North- Eastern Health Board are fortunate in having the service of such an experienced and caring obstetrician'.

One indication of our birthing culture is the fact that the three Dublin teaching hospitals, which cater for 40 per cent of the nation's births, are headed by clinical and organisational CEOs called 'Masters'. This is a system unique to Dublin and the *Independent Review of Maternity and Gynaecology Services in the Greater Dublin Area*, commissioned by the Health Service Executive (2008), says it's an inappropriate system in today's world. To appreciate how patriarchal are its underlying assumptions (with no disrespect to Masters past or present) imagine there being a 'Mistress' of a Dublin teaching hospital.

Since then, perhaps due to the increased empowerment of women, there has been a small return of the pendulum. There are 'domino' schemes, offering low-risk women midwife-led care in the Rotunda and National Maternity Hospitals in Dublin, and the Coombe Women's Hospital is developing midwife-led care. Cavan General Hospital and – by a nice coincidence – Our Lady of Lourdes Hospital, Drogheda, have midwife-led units.

Midwife-led care has proved successful, safe and cheap. The comparative intervention statistics for 2005 compiled by Cuidiú/ the Irish Childbirth Trust's show starkly how very different is the care available in the midwife-led units in Cavan and Drogheda from the care in consultant-led units: they have no epidurals, no instrumental deliveries and no induction of labour. Now of course these are low-risk mothers who have selected a low-tech option – but the fact that such a low level of intervention can be achieved is astonishing when we look at the level of intervention going on everywhere else.

Midwife-led care is the way that low-risk pregnancy management is going. *The Independent Review of Maternity and Gynaecology Services* in 2008 advocated more midwife-led units, more care in the community by midwives and the option of home birth, to bring Ireland into line with best practice internationally: 'International evidence clearly indicates that women should be offered choice. It is particularly obvious that there is significant potential for midwives to play a more prominent role in obstetrics.'

But the fact remains that in recent times most mothers have been processed fairly ruthlessly according to norms and schedules laid down by consultants, focused, as sociologist Jo Murphy-Lawless has shown in *Reading Birth and Death: a History of Obstetric Thinking* (1998) on preventing the deaths of mothers and infants, within a system in which huge numbers of mothers gave birth and there were limited resources. In this system the voice of the individual woman has nearly been lost.

Our National Maternity Hospital in Holles Street dreamed up and spread to many other countries a technique called 'active management of labour'. Its cornerstone is the use of oxytocic drugs to accelerate labour so that 'supply chain' management can be usefully applied. From the time of the diagnosis of labour, when a woman's cervix should be dilated to two centimetres or more, her progress is mapped on a graph called a 'partogram', which ends at ten centimetres' dilation. If she does not make adequate 'progress' towards the goal of delivery, her labour is accelerated by the use of drugs.

With active management you can predict the length of a labour, so you can manage scarce resources efficiently. It was a pretty rational response to limited resources by one of the busiest maternity hospitals in these islands, in a country where people tended to have lots of babies and it was ordained that every baby be born in a consultant-led hospital.

All the Irish hospitals practise some form of active management. In fact, active management as practised in its original form, at the National Maternity Hospital, may at times have advantages over the regime in other hospitals. The National Maternity Hospital is dedicated to maintaining a relatively low rate of Caesarean section: it was 18.3 per cent compared with 25.6 per cent in the Rotunda in 2005.

One of my friends had signed for a Caesarean section on her first baby at the Rotunda, after what she calls the 'spiral of intervention': the artificial rupture of her waters and an epidural. When she went into theatre she asked the staff to give her one more go and they agreed. Out came the baby. She says now:

> I had an awful lot of fear and the hospital fed that
> fear by giving me deadlines, which are completely
> unnatural and inappropriate. Their attitude was that
> I had to be mobilised and that ethos is ingrained
> in consultant-led care. And unfortunately, a lot of
> women want to be managed. They don't realise that
> having a baby in your own time is possibly the most
> empowering thing you can ever do in your life.

Active management of labour ensures that the woman loses control of her own experience. From the moment of her admission to the National Maternity Hospital, the manual, *Active Management of Labour*, now in its fourth edition, silences her. Diagnosis of labour should not be 'left to mothers', it says. From then on, she is slave to her 'partogram': 'In the National Maternity Hospital, prolonged labour was defined as thirty-six hours in 1963, reduced to twenty-four hours in 1968 and, finally, to twelve hours in 1972. A formal decision was taken on 1 January 1972 to restrict the duration of labour to twelve hours.

I'm moved to ask if the then Master communicated the change in policy to the babies of the future? Because some of them don't seem to have got the message. With active management, women are often subjected to interventions that they neither want nor need so that their partograms accord with hospital policy. While safety considerations coupled with economic considerations were undoubtedly to the fore in the development of active management, I can't help wondering if a deeper need to control women wasn't at play as well.

Control of labour is one of our cultural traditions. Jo Murphy Lawless explains that the predecessor of the Rotunda, the Lying-in Hospital for Poor Women, was the first dedicated maternity hospital in these islands. The Dublin School of Midwifery originated in the Rotunda and was the most influential school of obstetrics in these islands in the nineteenth century. The 'episiotomy', a surgical incision to the perinaeum to speed vaginal birth, was invented by the Rotunda's Fielding Ould and exported worldwide, although its effectiveness and the effect it has on women are still debated.

Can our high birth rate alone explain the extent of this contribution to obstetric practice? It may be the case that we also have a particularly strong need to control women in childbirth.

It is dangerous to ignore the voice of the woman. In 2010 a 'scanning scandal' came to light: seven women came forward to say that they had been advised to have D and C (dilation and curettage) procedures to empty the contents of their wombs, when a scan indicated that their babies were dead. Still feeling pregnant, they insisted on a second scan, which revealed a healthy baby.

At the National Maternity Hospital in 2000, my miscarriage was handled with huge sensitivity. I feel so lucky that I was offered a choice of a D and C or letting 'nature take its course' and that I chose the latter. A roll of black plastic sacks was needed to clear up the consequences.

It seems to be mostly to avoid mess, inconvenience and perhaps a second admission to hospital that D and C's have been routinely indicated after incomplete miscarriages. The procedure tidies up all that women's stuff. But it shouldn't happen on the basis of the diagnosis of one operator using one machine, particularly when the voice of the pregnant woman is ignored. Jo Murphy-Lawless was warning of the importance of a second scan a full twelve years ago after a misdiagnosed miscarriage in Cardiff.

Health analyst, writer and activist Marie O'Connor says, in an interview with me, that active management, developed at the National Maternity Hospital, was 'part of the repressive Catholic mindset of the 1950s'. Now spokesperson for the Survivors of Symphysiotomy group, she calls this brutal severing of a woman's pelvic joint to deliver a baby "the outer edge of active management".

This surgical procedure known as 'symphysiotomy' severs the cartilage of the pubis symphysis joint of the pelvis, allowing the pelvis to widen – permanently. It may have had an advantage over

Caesarean section in the eyes of Irish Catholic doctors in that it did not limit women's families as repeated Caesarean section would have done.

You can't have C-section after C-section. No more than three sections are advisable and it is only recently that vaginal birth after a section has been considered. But once symphysiotomy has opened the door, any number of babies can make their way out. The problem is that the mother may have difficulty walking, incontinence, pain, psychological problems and sexual problems for the rest of her life.

The operation was developed before Caesarean sections became relatively safe and is still performed in situations in which Caesarean sections are not possible. What has caused controversy is that it was performed in Ireland from the 1940s through to the 1980s, when Caesarean sections were both possible and relatively safe. The procedure was revived in the National Maternity Hospital in 1944 by the then Master, Alex Spain. It was promoted by the next Master, Arthur Barry, a firm opponent of 'artificial' birth control. Marie O'Connor is convinced that it was favoured over the Caesarean section because it did not limit women's families or encourage them to use contraception.

It was also much practised by Gerard Connolly, one of the founding consultants at Our Lady of Lourdes Hospital, Drogheda. This was, says Marie O'Connor, 'quite a schizophrenic unit', with Connolly apparently attempting to maximise women's families and Michael Neary putting an end to them: 'The only constant', says O'Connor, 'was male consultant power and female powerlessness.'

There are a hundred and fifty survivors of the procedure in contact with Survivors of Symphysiotomy, but more than 1500 procedures are known to have been carried out. The operation was performed in hospitals all over Ireland. O'Connor is convinced that the hospitals were using the women as guinea pigs because they were training doctors for the African missions, where the hospital conditions necessary for C-section might not have been available. The Irish women were sometimes not told they had the operation, even when they were discharged after ten or twelve days in hospital and were not able to walk. Often, their GPs were not informed.

The survivors have been refused a full enquiry in this country. O'Connor says that, if necessary, they will go to the UN in their search for justice.

The reason that I find these stories of women's powerlessness during childbirth so compelling is that I have experienced powerlessness during childbirth myself. No major harm done. But let's just say that empathy is not a problem for me when it comes to the hysterectomy and symphysiotomy victims.

I had a short, powerful labour with my first baby, Jack, at the National Maternity Hospital in 1999. I had been made aware of the potential side-effects of epidural – headaches, backaches, instrumental delivery – and I decided to avoid it if I could.

I found the whole experience spectacularly painful. It didn't feel 'natural' at all. It felt like a mistake. For a start, my baby seemed to have lost his compass and be coming out of my bum. But when Jack was born! I never thought I would see gain in pain, but after the pain of childbirth the body rushes to heal itself and I experienced the biggest high of my life. All night long I lay beside Jack, wondering at how I knew his little movements already from carrying him in the womb. I said, 'We'll always be good friends, Jack,' and so we have been.

The birth of Tom and Ino was always going to be different. A pilot programme of midwife-led care by community midwives had just begun at the National Maternity Hospital and I opted to go with them, until I was diagnosed with twins and had to leave the scheme. I opted for private care in the hope that in a private room I might get some rest.

I was told that every effort would be made to avoid Caesarean section but the labour itself was never discussed with me, so that, when I went into sudden, swift labour at thirty-eight weeks and arrived in the labour ward, I didn't have any idea what to expect. Immediately I was put under pressure to have an epidural. With my husband's support, I withstood the pressure as long as I could, then caved in. In hindsight, the epidural may well have been a good idea. Ino was a breech baby and had to be pulled out. I might well have had to have an emergency Caesarean and the epidural would already have been in place.

But I knew none of these things. I just felt bullied. And then I felt numb from the waist down. I lay as powerless as a moth with a pin through it, as my two little men came into the world. I did not experience pain but I did not experience labour either. And afterwards, I experienced no high.

When I went back to look at my notes I found they stated, 'Epidural requested'.

My labours were getting faster and faster. With Tom and Ino I was fine one minute and the next minute I was in full labour. Now I believe that my womb was so distended – between them, the babies weighed fourteen pounds – that I didn't feel early labour at all. With Róise, my third pregnancy, I assumed I would have an even more shockingly fast labour. That's why I opted for a home birth with the community midwives at the National Maternity Hospital. It wasn't that I had a particular desire to give birth at home; I just didn't want to end up giving birth in a car.

The midwife-led ante-natal care was amazing. I was meeting women dressed in civvies who treated me like an equal. I remember one midwife apologising to me that I might be kept waiting for a few minutes and advising me to go for coffee. They visited me at home and the three little boys got to listen to the baby in Mummy's tummy.

I didn't understand that I was still part of the great active management machine.

I rang the midwives the minute I felt my labour stirring, because, as I had told them many times, I was terrified of going into a rapid labour and giving birth unaided. The midwife on duty arrived promptly and asked me about my 'contractions'. They were frequent enough but not painful, so I believe I was not in labour at all, just having the tremors called Braxton Hicks contractions, which many women get at various stages before they go into labour. 'Without pain,' says the active management manual, 'the question of labour simply does not arise.' And I would agree with this.

But the midwife examined me, found me to be two centimetres dilated and pronounced that I was in labour. From that moment, I was on the partogram and could not escape.

When I went back to discuss my labour with the Community Midwife Manager, Margaret Hanahoe, she said she might wait till a woman was three centimetres dilated – or even four – before diagnosing labour. I had twins the year before and might have been two centimetres dilated before I started. But I was stuck on the chart and having a few mild Braxton Hicks while my husband made tea for the midwife. We are very hospitable people and we felt bad that we were not able to put on a good show. But I wasn't in labour and there wasn't anything I could do about it. I just wanted to go to bed.

It was when I suggested this that I understood my number was up. 'You've started now and you'll have to continue,' said the midwife. She broke my waters in an effort to get things going but not much happened. Next, as my notes state, she declared that I 'needed oxytocin to accelerate labour' and would have to go to hospital. An ambulance was called and we went off like lambs to the slaughter.

The rest I had in the ambulance and a break from the pressure of trying to be a good hostess were a help. I started to say that I felt I was going into labour but I wasn't listened to. I was sitting on a bed in a labour ward in the early morning, with medical staff ranged all around me. They told me they'd have my epidural arranged in a jiffy but I refused to have one. They said I needed oxytocin and I said I didn't.

I had already begun the research which would lead to this book so I had a fair idea what I was talking about. I remember sitting there saying, 'Active management is controversial.' It is so interesting that my articulate, analytical self could say whatever she liked but my labouring self was powerless. In hindsight, the most terrifying moment was when I asked them *why* they thought I needed the oxytocin and there was an awful pause. They looked at one another with all the appearance of *not knowing why*. Then somebody said, 'In the past, women had endless labours.' That was as far as the explanation went. 'It's just your natural hormone,' I was told and I was put on the drip.

I felt my first serious contraction but the nurse said, 'The oxytocin hasn't hit yet.' My body was going into a naturally strong labour and then the oxytocin entered my system. I went off like a firecracker. I was completely out of control and squealing like a pig as I knelt on the hard tiles of the labour ward. I dilated the whole way in about half an hour. The baby burst out of me and was pronounced a girl but I was screaming until after the placenta was delivered.

'Ah,' said somebody, 'that's the jungle juice.'

To echo Harding Clark, nobody died. In fact, nobody suffered any lasting physical damage. As soon as I stopped screaming, I delighted in my beautiful baby girl and I had her in a sling at the school gate a few days later. But I will never forget the horror of that labour.

In stark contrast to the way in which many consultants and obstetricians have tended to behave when questioned, Margaret Hanahoe of the Community Midwives' Scheme met me to review my chart earlier this year and was straight with me. She made the point that hospital policy had been adhered to in my case. But the whole 'success' of active management hinges on accurate diagnosis of labour.

'If you feel yourself it was because you were never in labour in the first place…well, you're the one who was experiencing it,' she says, but does not argue with the midwife's diagnosis, which would have been based not just on dilation but on factors such as the effacement of the cervix, the regularity of the contractions and where the baby's head was in relation to the pelvis and cervix.

I have a wonderful relationship with my only daughter but I hope, if she ever has a child, that she will not go through what I went through having her.

# 8

## DRY UP: WHY BREAST ISN'T BEST IN IRELAND

*'Why do people in modern, industrialised societies feel disturbed by seeing a suckling mother and baby? Perhaps they are experiencing powerful unconscious feelings from their own infancy. Many adults around today would not have experienced the kind of cuddly, responsive babyhood that is now known to influence the development of the emotional sector of our brains. Most breastfeeding cultures unthinkingly provided close physical contact and immediate comfort to meet a baby's needs. In societies where leaving babies to cry and physically separating them from their mothers are culturally acceptable, parents can be extremely tense and nervous. Consequently, many of us babies have experienced sadness too early in life, well before we could understand or cope with it. Babies tend to be viewed as insensate beings or even loathed.*

Gabrielle Palmer, *The Politics of Breastfeeding: When Breasts are Bad for Business*

'It's cheap and convenient,' said my mother grimly, when I started to breastfeed my first child. Even at the time I thought she was doing battle with big feelings. That she was offering me an explanation I could use for breastfeeding so that I wouldn't have to admit to an intimate love affair with the child at my breast.

My mother had breast-fed us three children, the eldest for five months, the youngest – me – for three. She said she did it because of the example of a very advanced friend, a *Manchester Guardian* reader like herself. But she started her life as a mother when she had my brother in the 1940s. Breastfeeding really only collapsed in Ireland in the late 1950s. Although I was, it seems, fed at the breast, I did not have the benefit of unlimited contact with my mother's body. My mother used to tell me that when the very austere Auntie May asked her what she needed to feed her baby, she asked for a clock. She went upstairs with the clock and fed the baby for whatever was the fashionable number of minutes on each breast.

'It worked,' she said, but I wonder if it did. None of us was breast-fed for all that long and the great unknown is how many 'supplementary' bottles we got. I know that when my mother had her first baby, a maid used to bath the baby every morning and bring him in to my mother for his feed. For a mother like me who spent half the night listening to playbacks on RTÉ as the baby suckled on and on, this seems quite incredible. She herself found it incredible from today's perspective and remembered with surprise that she and her very advanced friend used to complain that they had to give the children their tea on a Wednesday because it was their maids' day off.

They were both women in their twenties married to journalists in their twenties, living in rented flats in Dublin. They didn't have any family money. I suppose there were enough women who were worse off than them and happy to take the few shillings my mother and her friend had to spare for the lowly work of nursing a baby.

There were no maids by the time I came along but there was Annie. When I was little I thought everyone had an Annie. I remember drawing pictures of Mummy, Daddy and Annie. I loved colouring Annie's orange hair. Annie was from Galway, a staunch Catholic and the maker of endless cakes of brown bread, tea brack and apple tarts. She minded me every morning from when I was born until I went to school, and I am sure that Annie bottle-fed me even when I was meant to be a breast-fed baby.

Annie would have found it impossible to leave me crying because she was kindness personified. She was unable to have children herself – she said she 'had God annoyed' with asking –

and she probably invested a lot of her spare love in me. Every time I went out the door Annie showered her little black Protestant with Holy Water and said, "Twill do you no harm, anyway." Nor did it. I have no doubt that Annie's love-charms are still working for me.

She regularly brought me with her to Communion at Mass. I have never had that fear of Catholicism which many Protestants have, which shows how bringing someone from outside the family into a child's life can be a big advantage.

When I went to see her with my first baby, Jack, she met me at the door with the words, 'Don't put him in a crèche, give him to a mother.' She continued on this theme throughout the visit, even to the point of offering to mind him herself, although she was elderly and lived miles from me. Perhaps Annie is the real source of my love of children.

I've been told that I probably breast-fed my children because my mother fed me and it may be true. But I find it hard to make the connection between what my mother described as controlled, clock-watching feeding and my own experience.

When I was a teenager I worked abroad as an au-pair for a family in which there was a three-month-old baby. I fell in love with her. I had never 'known' a baby before and I had been hired to look after the older children. But this baby's mother was having none of her. I suppose she had post-natal depression. The baby would scream and scream for her bottle and it used to break my heart because I didn't know how to make it.

I would be sent down to the beach with the baby and the older children. It still makes my blood run cold to think of it. The beach would be black with people and I was always losing the children, which meant I had to leave my station under the umbrella beside the baby and go and look for them. I hated to leave the baby's side. And then, on the rare occasions when I had time off, I found myself longing for her. I have no doubt now but that nature orchestrated the whole relationship. The baby was in peril because her mother was off the job so I was recruited.

The part of this that I find most interesting now is that I used

to love to hold the baby against my skin and I would take off my
T-shirt to do it. I realised this was slightly off-colour because the
baby was not 'mine' and in any case, I didn't want to be caught
without my T-shirt on. I'm sure I was prompted by deep instincts
to hold the baby close.

I don't know if I was 'naturally' a very maternal person or if
that experience of minding that baby was the thing that swayed
me. What I do know is that I always intended to have children and
always intended to breast-feed. It wasn't just that I knew it was
best for the baby. I wanted the experience of closeness.

There is a great lie implicit in my mother's simple comparison
between breastfeeding and bottle-feeding for their cheapness
and convenience. The truth is that giving a child the breast is a
life-changing experience for women. A woman's mind is literally
changed by giving birth and breastfeeding changes it still further.
It creates new neural pathways which lead to what primatologist
Sarah Blaffer Hrdy, in *Mother Nature*, calls 'the reorganisation of
the mother's brain'.

What is it that makes us seek to deny this transformation? I
think our whole culture is imbued with a fear of the female and
there is nothing more completely female than a pregnant or
breastfeeding woman. We fear the unknown and the uncanny
– Freud's *unheimlich*. A pregnant or breastfeeding woman is
changed by forces outside herself and greater than herself. We fear
her. We fear her even if we are her.

My mother's simple comparison also masked another
troubling fact, which is that breastfeeding, with the 'let-down'
governed by the love hormone, oxytocin, is a sensual experience
for a woman. As Hrdy puts it:

> Some women – as well as men – are unnerved
> by what they perceive as the 'sexual' sensations
> mothers experience during breastfeeding. Tales
> abound of officials at public welfare agencies who
> react negatively to maternal confessions about
> sensual feelings from nursing their children. Some

go so far as to seek removal of the offspring from so 'perverting' an influence. It might be helpful for all concerned to keep in mind that maternal sensations have clear evolutionary priority in the pleasure sphere. Long before any woman found sexual foreplay or intercourse pleasurable, her ancestors were selected to respond positively to similar sensations produced by birth and suckling, because finding these activities pleasurable would help condition her in ways that kept her infant alive. It would be more nearly correct, then, to refer to the 'afterglow' from climax as an ancient 'maternal' rather than sexual response.

Prolactin, the hormone that controls milk production and is present in all women who give birth regardless of whether they breastfeed or not, acts on the brain like a natural opiate. It is associated with maternal behaviour in a wide range of animals and some birds. Women who did not wish to breastfeed in Ireland used to be routinely injected with a drug that suppressed prolactin and may have curbed women's enjoyment of their babies. Economist Finola Kennedy, who gave birth in the 1960s, remembers a nun offering her 'something to dry you up'.

Is it just me who finds the idea of these routine injections to curb a woman's mothering instinct absolutely terrifying? All the more so when you remember that Michael Neary attributed his need to take out the wombs of some women to the lactation suppressants taken by their mothers.

Caitriona Clear argues convincingly that Irish women gave up breastfeeding because they wanted to. She quotes statistics showing that even in the 1940s the breastfeeding rate was much higher in the UK than it was in Ireland. But you have to ask why Irishwomen wanted to give it up: were they isolated because feeding openly was not accepted, expected to get on with agricultural work when they had young babies or convinced that the bottle was the future?

The HSE's *National Infant Feeding Survey*, 2008, collated statistics which showed Irish breastfeeding rates declining from 64 per cent in the 1950s to 16 per cent by 1975. The researchers, from the School of Nursing and Midwifery at TCD, found that the breastfeeding rate is increasing, from 36 per cent in 1999 to 44 per cent in 2005, but caution that new data collection methods may have queered the results.

Of one thing we can be sure: we have the lowest breastfeeding rate in Europe and probably in the developed world.

More breastfeeding seems to have survived in other countries even if long-term breastfeeding was abandoned; the Norwegians nearly all continued to breast-feed for the first couple of months even through the 1950s and 1960s, so that restoring the breast-feeding rate in that country wasn't the battle it has been here. Asked why we abandoned it wholesale, Ireland's Breastfeeding Coordinator, Maureen Fallon, wonders whether our relative poverty may have made us more susceptible to marketing. In those days formula could be freely advertised and formula-feeding was promoted in hospitals.

But that's history. What is surprising is that today, when there is such strong medical evidence for the advantages of breastfeeding and official medical support, so many Irish women still don't do it.

Maureen Fallon is Ireland's first Breastfeeding Coordinator, appointed on foot of a recommendation of the Innocenti Declaration (1990), in which thirty governments and ten UN agencies called for a radical approach to create a global breast-feeding culture. She was converted to the cause of breastfeeding by Maori women when she was working in New Zealand: 'I would tell them what to do if they didn't have enough milk and they hooted with laughter. I had trained in Queen Charlotte's Hospital in London and I was meant to have all the knowledge. It was like a blinding light.'

In the nine years she has held the job the number of women who start breastfeeding has steadily gone up. But when I spoke to her she was disheartened and about to take early retirement:

> If I were to say one thing about Ireland by com-
> parison with other countries I would have to say that
> the white coats have not supported breastfeeding in
> the way that they should have. In any country where
> breastfeeding has really taken off, there was no
> equivocation. The paediatricians and obstetricians
> are leading out on it. Here it's a case of, 'Oh yes, you
> should breastfeed, but...' There's nearly always a
> 'but': 'But if you don't it's OK.' You may as well say,
> 'Don't bother.' We should be unequivocal that
> breastfeeding is the norm for babies in Ireland.
> Not, oh, it's the best and we strive to do it but if we
> don't it's OK. Choice suggests that it's between two
> reasonably equal alternatives and that's not the case.

Before I had my first baby, the advantages of breastfeeding
were listed to me by the National Maternity Hospital midwife
with whom I did my excellent (private) ante-natal course. The
National Infant Feeding Survey 2008 says that breast-fed infants
suffer less 'morbidity' from gastrointestinal and respiratory
infections, fewer urinary tract infections, fewer ear infections and
less eczema, asthma and rhinoconjunctivitis (although the degree
of this protection is under question).

Pre-term babies are less likely to die if they are breast-fed.

Children who are breast-fed are less likely to develop early-
onset diabetes. They have less risk of developing Hodgkin's
disease and possibly leukaemia. In adulthood, having been
breast-fed lowers your chances of developing Type 2 diabetes,
raised blood pressure and obesity.

Mothers who breastfeed will be likely to return to their
pre-pregnancy weight more quickly and have less chance of
developing pre-menopausal breast cancer, ovarian cancer and
osteoporosis. Irish rates of all these adult illnesses are among the
highest in Europe, yet I have never heard anyone link this to the
fact that so many of today's middle-aged people were not breast-
fed and the women have not breast-fed their own babies.

I can't believe that the many Irish mothers who clearly understand the advantages of breastfeeding and who are fully supported by committed medical staff would *choose* formula. But the marketing of formula goes on apace. As I researched this chapter I was being urged, on prime-time television, to buy Aptamil's 'follow-on' milk.

There is no need for 'follow-on milk'. If you're not breast-feeding you can feed your baby formula for a year, then switch to cow's milk. Gabrielle Palmer reports that 'Follow-on milks' have been described as 'unnecessary products' by the WHO

These advertisements break the World Health Assembly's 1981 International Code of Marketing of Breastmilk Substitutes. They are marketing a breastmilk substitute, as the WHO recommendation for breastfeeding is that it should continue for two years and beyond. Follow-on milks were devised to get around the restrictions on the marketing of formula to babies under six months and are intended to reach women whose babies are younger than this. A survey in the UK revealed that one in five women had introduced follow-on milk to their babies at younger than three months, although the milks are a health risk to babies under six months.

Then there is the more subtle level of the advertisement. The breastfeeding woman is grounded, while the bottle-feeding woman gets out in the sunshine. *The National Infant Feeding Survey,* 2008, clearly shows that embarrassment at breastfeeding in public is *still* a major fact in Irish women giving up. The survey found that less than 49 per cent of Irish breast-feeders had breast-fed in public, while over 63 per cent of breast-feeders living in Ireland but from other ethnic groups had breast-fed in public.

Meanwhile the medical authorities, as if afraid to speak like adults to women in a 'fragile and emotional state', confine themselves to a few gentle prompts to breastfeed. And then sabotage the often desperate efforts of those who try.

The Baby Friendly Hospital Initiative is a global campaign by the World Health Organisation and the United Nations Children's Fund which aims to implement in maternity hospitals the best practice that supports breastfeeding. There are about 19,000 recognised Baby Friendly Hospitals in the world.

The Baby Friendly initiative was launched in Ireland in 1998. The first Irish hospitals to reach Baby Friendly standard were Portiuncula Hospital, Ballinasloe, and Waterford Regional Hospital. The only other hospitals that have reached the standard in any year are St Munchin's Regional Maternity Hospital, Limerick, the Rotunda Hospital, Dublin and University Hospital, Galway, Our Lady of Lourdes, Drogheda, and Cavan General Hospital.

Dr Genevieve Becker, a lactation consultant and researcher, is employed by the HSE the grand total of fifty days a year to drive the Baby Friendly Initiative in Ireland. When asked why adequate resources have never been put into supporting breastfeeding, she says, 'Because we don't value children in this country. When you value children as the future of a country then you value their mothers and all the pieces fall into place.'

I didn't know to check on the National Maternity Hospital's Baby Friendly status before I rolled up to have my first baby in 1999. I had done work as a journalist on the hospital's excellent arts programme and some of my colleagues in *The Irish Times* had their babies there. It was the nearest hospital to me. That's pretty much the only criterion for most women.

A couple of the midwives were definitely iffy about breast-feeding. One midwife said, 'Breastfeeding is great – when it works.' Another kept wanting to give the baby a bottle of water which would have reduced his desire to suckle and so reduced my supply, or even led to an inability to suck at the breast.

I didn't know that WHO/UNICEF had published *Ten Steps to Successful Breastfeeding* and that the midwife was in conflict with Item 6, 'Give newborn infants no food or drink other than breastmilk unless medically indicated,' and Item 9, 'Give no artificial teats or pacifiers (also called dummies or soothers) to breastfeeding infants.'

But I fended off the nurse with my baby care manual, Penelope Leach's *Your Baby and Child*. For some reason – probably because she had been the guru of my boss at *The Irish Times* – I believed everything she said. I believed I should breastfeed and more importantly, I believed I *could* breastfeed. I fought off the bottle and I fought off the desperation I felt because my baby never stopped crying. I would have been more desperate still had I known he wasn't going to stop for four months.

I was the only mother breastfeeding in the ward. As my baby wailed behind the curtain, I heard the other mothers showing off their sleeping infants to admiring guests. 'I considered breastfeeding...' one woman kept saying, with the sound track from my young Jack supplying the rest of the sentence: 'But I'm glad I decided against it.' One mother, who worked for a formula company, gave me the only bit of support. 'They say bottle-feeding makes them less intelligent,' she said, as she offered her baby the teat.

'He couldn't be hungry *again*,' I said to one of the midwives. 'Could,' she replied simply. She was my breastfeeding saviour. She had a saying which I think sums up the challenge that breastfeeding presents to modern Irish women: 'What else would you be doing?'

What else? Sorting the socks, reading Proust, doing tax returns...So much to do!

But only one infancy for every baby. Only one chance.

When I was just about to leave the hospital and go out into the big, bad world, Jack – trussed up in his bodysuit and car seat – started to cry. I was all for pressing on with my agenda. Get out. Get on. I hadn't yet learned that babies change plans.

My breastfeeding saviour arrived and called a spade a spade: 'He's roaring,' she announced. She would help me with the impossible task of getting him out of the seat and out of his suit and 'latched on'. I found this so hard to do that listening to him cry was nearly easier.

He latched on. He fed. I went out into the big, blue yonder.

Maureen Fallon doesn't like my story. 'People say, "I was lucky to find the right midwife. *But it shouldn't be luck.* That absolutely goes to my very soul.'

Although I did what Penelope Leach said and let Jack feed whenever he wanted to, he was hungry most of the time. I know he was probably just a hungry baby but I also think I lactated badly. I remember my husband taking the baby for a spin around College Green because I quite simply had nothing more to give. One weekend I went to bed with the baby for thirty-six hours, declaring what Leach calls a 'breastfeeding emergency'. I remember the sun splitting the stones outside my bedroom window.

One morning when he was four months old I strode up to the supermarket, bought some baby porridge and stuffed it into him. Then and only then did he stop roaring. I was very relieved. But the struggle to breastfeed had certainly been worth it because I kept feeding him outside work hours for two years. This massively reduced the stress I felt when I went back to work and I feel it must have helped him too.

By the time I had my twin boys, Tom and Ino, two years later, I had become a radical. The experience of fighting off the bottles of water – not to mention the bottle of sugary formula suggested by another health professional – had radicalised me. Up until then it would never have occurred to me that the health services would tell me to do something that was bad for my health or for my baby's health. I had total faith in them.

But I knew going in that I would have to fight to feed Tom and Ino and I was ready for it. Penelope Leach said you could do it and there was even a picture of breast-fed twins in Your Baby and Child. I met breast-fed twins once in my doctor's surgery. A friend's Canadian partner had fed her twins and had sent me a special cushion.

I went in armed. But I hadn't reckoned on the public ward. I had opted for private care simply to get a room of my own, away from all the other wailing babies. But I didn't get it for the first two nights, so there I was, in the corner of a big ward, lifting the starving babies one after the other into my narrow bed. My saviour midwife arrived again – sent by God – and tried to set me up to feed them at the same time on a bank of pillows but the bed was so narrow I was worried they would fall off.

I remember a pretty midwife, her hair cascading out of her cap, who took a dim view of Tom's progress. His initial birth weight had not been very high and she was watching him. But I knew he was doing fine.

'How long has he fed?' she kept asking me. Like I was timing him! He was feeding. I just knew he was feeding.

'We'll have to take him away and test his blood sugar,' she said menacingly.

'What will you do if you get a bad result?' I asked.

'Give him a bottle,' she said quickly.

'I thought you'd try to get him feeding better, or use expressed milk,' I said, to which she replied something like, 'Oh yes, all of that...'

His blood sugar was fine.

When I got the call to go across to the private wing, the private nurses asked the pretty midwife if I was 'breast or bottle?'

'Breast,' she told them and made a face.

The handover from public to private was absurd in itself. One carpet ran out and another began. The baby was switched from one kind of crib to another. It was like a war-time meeting of generals.

My lunch, which had been put down in front of me in the public ward, then whipped away because I was about to go to private, was finally replaced and I fell on it as if I had never seen food before.

But whereas I was to go private, the twins were to go public. 'We do four-hourly feeds,' announced the nurse. I was stunned. No newborn breast-fed baby does four-hourly feeds. Breast-fed babies should choose their own *private* feeding times or else they will not develop their own *private* milk supply. Step 8 in the WHO/UNICEF *Ten Steps to Successful Breastfeeding* is, 'Encourage breastfeeding on demand.'

A part of me was thinking, 'Could all this work be over? Should I just sink back on the cushions here and let them take the babies away?'

This was the part of me which was being serviced by the private wing. I was the paying client, after all – not the babies. There was widespread dismay among the nurses that I was not 'getting my sleep'. I did not expect to 'get my sleep' as I had newborn, breast-fed twin boys. My special feeding cushion from Canada, a firm, foam semi-circle, was being admired by the staff, who said they had never seen one before. The babies were feeding together, one at each breast, in what is called a 'football hold' and it was magic. When I think of the alternative, which might have left one of them roaring while the other was bottle-fed or both of them somehow propped up so that two bottles could be administered at once – and that's two sterilised bottles of freshly made-up formula – I am sick with anger at what happened next.

The nurses were coming in to me during the night to help me to latch the babies on. I welcomed their company and support. But it soon became clear that they thought I was mad.

During the second feed of the night one nurse leant close, looked me in the eyes, and said, 'Would you not consider combined feeding?'

I told her to leave. To introduce bottles at that point would probably have marked the end of my breastfeeding. The babies would not have been hungry enough to suckle enough to produce enough milk. Bit by bit my supply would have ebbed away and the bottle would have taken over.

'Show me a woman who's using bottles and I'll show you a woman who won't be breastfeeding in a matter of weeks,' says Maureen Fallon.

Worse still, because the technique of sucking is so different at a breast from at a bottle, the babies could forget how to suckle and refuse the breast outright.

The suggestion broke so many of the *Steps to Successful Breastfeeding* that it demolished the staircase.

I knew I was right but I was made to feel like a freak. At some stage the next day another nurse came in, gave me a look and said, 'You're the one who won't take the bottles.'

Going by the nurses' station at night, I heard a nurse say, 'I just don't *understand* anyone who gives no bottles.'

No doubt she was telling no more than the truth. She didn't understand. The paediatrician with whom the twins had their expensive, private six-week check-up asked me how much food they were 'taking' and when I said they were breast-fed he made a face.

I breast-fed my twins for a year. Women are given the equipment to feed twins and it's interesting that I never had the supply problems with Tom and Ino that I had with Jack. I think my body just got better at it. I felt fantastic. I briefly developed an hour-glass figure which I made every effort to show off. My princelings had made me a princess.

I was high as a kite and I wonder now if this was because I had a twin dose of the love hormone, oxytocin, racing through my body. Whatever happened, I was pregnant again ten months later. Perhaps I am a biological curiosity because breastfeeding has never had any effect on my fertility.

I weaned the babies because number four was on the way and I didn't want there to be a scrum at the breast. I wish they had had more breastfeeding, particularly Tom, who turned out to be autistic. David Tammet, who has Asperger syndrome, has written about the importance of breastfeeding to autistic people: the security, the communication, the experience of touch.

Looking back, I am glad that any advantages in brain development which breastfeeding offers were Tom's for at least for the first year. But if I had known then what I know now, I would have kept him feeding along with his baby sister for at least another year.

Life isn't like that, though. You can't go back and change the bits you don't like. What you can do is learn from the mistakes of the past. My last baby, Róise, was breast-fed for more than four years. This might sound extreme to the uninitiated but breast-feeding naturally reduces so that for a toddler it's more a case of the odd swig. This means your child can always, always be comforted, even in extreme distress or illness. I used to call the breast my 'nuclear option'.

It would be one thing if all the women who bottle-feed their babies in Ireland had chosen to do so. But many want to breastfeed and 'fail'. 'Breastfeeding failure' is such a terrible expression. It means that the method doesn't work, of course, not that the woman is a failure. But you can be sure the woman will feel like one.

*The National Infant Feeding Survey* found that 81 per cent of mothers who had switched from breastfeeding to formula feeding by three to four months wanted to breastfeed for longer. Some mothers may carry that sadness for years.

For many women 'breastfeeding failure' happens in hospital. Genevieve Becker tells me that between 'breastfeeding initiation' and discharge from hospital, about 3500 mothers are 'lost' to breastfeeding. The shocking truth is that the longer a mother stays in an Irish hospital, the less likely she is to be fully breastfeeding at discharge.

If the support for breastfeeding isn't there in hospital, with round-the-clock nursing care, what hope do Irish mothers have?

For ever more, those women must live with the steady trickle of scientific evidence giving breast-fed babies more and more advantages. Of course, particularly in a First World country like Ireland, it is very likely that their children will be relatively healthy but women will always suspect that they could have been healthier if they were breast-fed. And if their children aren't healthy, they will blame themselves, even if the ill-health has nothing to do with their method of feeding.

*And the fact that they did not breastfeed is not their fault.*

Sorry for the italics, but this is something that drives me mad. Forget about the babies for a moment. Think of the mothers who feel like 'failures'.

The mothers who want to bottle-feed from the start are a different group completely. Becker says the health services should concentrate their efforts on women who want to breastfeed and support them in the early stages. These women will promote breastfeeding to other women if it works for them.

I have many friends whose breastfeeding has gone wrong in

hospital. One, whose first baby was born at the Coombe, Dublin, describes how, due to poor positioning, she fed her baby on 'running sores'. The ghastly experiment lasted three weeks. Her second child was delivered at home by an independent midwife and she fed him without any problem for two years.

The type of birth a woman has also has an impact on her ability to feed her baby. A HSE report reveals that while breastfeeding mothers who had a 'natural' delivery had an 84 per cent breastfeeding rate at discharge, those who had a vacuum or Caesarean delivery had a 72 per cent rate at discharge – a rate which I would see as a testament to the women's courage.

In general terms, says Becker, how the mother is treated during the birth experience will impact on whether she breast-feeds or not: 'How she feels about herself affects how she feels about breastfeeding.'

She refers to the effects of 'patriarchy': 'There's two things that men can't do that women can. Breastfeed and give birth. They've nearly taken away breastfeeding and they've done their best to take away birth too.'

She also refers to the prudish aversion to breastfeeding. She remembers a quote from a Scottish research study of young mothers, one of whom said, 'Only a pervert would put a baby's mouth on their breast.'

The Junior Certificate science textbook of fifteen years ago, she says, didn't include the ability to make milk as one of the definitions of a mammal. Those students are today's parents. And now, we virtually ignore parenting in the school curricula. The only mention of breastfeeding is in the childcare module of the Leaving Certificate Home Economics course.

Is it that we think that mentioning children will encourage the young people to go and make them? Which would be a disaster, wouldn't it? I remember a family friend worrying openly that because I was a freelance journalist I would not have access to maternity leave and my mother telling her not to give me any ideas. I think I was twenty-five at the time. It's not surprising it was ten more years before I had a baby.

It may be that the old fear of illegitimacy and the new fear of loss of independence are not really unrelated?

The shame is that fear of the loss of independence has led feminism, at times, to target breastfeeding. Betty Friedan saw an emphasis on breastfeeding as part of *The Feminine Mystique* but, in fact, breastfeeding initiation had reduced by half in the US in the years 1946 to 1956

Gabrielle Palmer references Arlie Russell Hochschild's study showing that 'the more that childcare and family life are made into a bundle of commodities and services to be bought and sold, the more the mother image is glorified.' (Palmer, p. 354) Friedan's problem was not, in fact, a society devoted to motherhood but a society devoted to spending.

Unfortunately our feminism, which tends to individualism, has also attacked breastfeeding. In Ireland, journalist Brenda Power minimised the advantages of breastfeeding in an influential article in *The Sunday Tribune* in 1999 and wrote that it was 'no coincidence' that the advantages of breastfeeding began to be stressed just when women were climbing 'the career ladder.'

This suggestion is easily challenged by the example of countries like Norway, whose women are among the richest and most powerful in the world and 98-99 per cent of whom breastfeed if they become mothers.

What is clear is that the rejection of breastfeeding is entrenched in Irish culture in a special way. The *NIFS* shows that Irish women are consistently outshone as breast-feeders by mothers from other countries who give birth in the same hospitals. Still more telling is the fact that although Northern Ireland has a British health system, its breastfeeding rate at 52 per cent initiation, is more Irish than British, a full 20 percentage points behind the rest of the UK.

We have a problem with motherhood. We have a problem with children. Is it any wonder that we can deny the importance of breastfeeding?

Nutritionist and campaigner Gabrielle Palmer estimates that more than 3000 babies die worldwide every day from infections caused by the lack of breastfeeding: the use of bottles, artificial milks and 'other risky products'.

Even in the First World, babies die for these reasons. In 1989 the US National Institute of Environmental Health Sciences estimated that four in every 1000 American babies died because they were not breast-fed. The risk of developing several potentially fatal conditions are increased by not breastfeeding and some of these babies die, even in Ireland.

But we continue with the attitude, summed up by the comment of one of the bottle-feeders quoted in the *NIFS*: 'A child never died on formula, either.'

The main disadvantage breastmilk has over infant formula is that it is not sold. A mother would never keep it from her baby until she got paid so she gives it freely. This means that although it makes people happy and healthy, it makes no one rich.

This is why it must be replaced.

We have been farming only for one per cent of human history, and we have been producing cow's milk surpluses only in relatively recent times. So it is in recent times that we have had to create a market for all that extra cow's milk where there was none before: part of that market is human babies.

Ireland is one of the world's leading exporters of infant formula. In the Food Safety Authority newsletter in 2007 there was an article about our formula industry under the unintentionally ironic title, 'Ireland – a natural source of infant nutrition.' How in the name of God could anyone call cow's milk a 'natural source' of nutrition for a human baby?

The article begins:

> Over the last two decades, Ireland has become one of the world's leading producers of infant nutritionals with the presence in Ireland of leading infant nutrition manufacturers – Wyeth, Abbott and Nutricia. The combined output from these companies accounts for almost 15 per cent of the world's powdered infant formula. Ireland's unique grass-

based production system makes it a natural location
for the industry and enables close collaboration
between dairy producers and industry.

Irish infant formula is exported to many countries, including
some in which many people do not have the resources to make
up formula with relative safety. The safety standards with regard
to the making-up of infant formula have risen higher and higher.
In 2007 new guidelines were launched by the WHO due to a new
understanding that infant formula is not a sterile substance. In
particular there is a danger with a bacterium called enterobacter
sakazakii, which can be life-threatening to an infant. It has been
associated with neonatal meningitis, necrotising enterocolitis,
bacteraemia and necrotising enterocolitis. Necrotising enterocolitis has a high mortality rate of 10-55 per cent, and meningitis
has a mortality rate of 40-80 per cent.

Cases of these infections are very rare. But to be really sure
your formula is made up safely, you have to wash your hands with
hot, soapy water, boil clean water, mix it with the powder in a
sterile bottle, let the mixture cool to 70 degrees and then feed with
a sterile teat. The WHO recommends using a 'sterilised forceps' to
handle the sterile equipment.

Can you imagine it? 'Make yourself a cup of tea, I'll be with
you in a second. I just have to sterilise my forceps.'

All unused formula should be thrown away after two hours,
before the procedure begins again.

In a clean, high-tech, Irish kitchen with a constant supply
of electricity, a clock and a thermometer, it would be hard to
implement these guidelines. In most homes in the world, it would
be impossible.

We Irish have our eye on China as the best new market for
our formula. China, as we know, is 'modernising' rapidly and
while some Chinese homes don't have the resources to make up
formula, others do. All right, it costs a fortune – Gabrielle Palmer
reckoned that feeding one baby on Mead Johnson formula costs
a third of a blue-collar wage in China – but it's seen as worth it to

adapt to the ways of the west. What a relief to get away from the Chinese breastmilk that has fed Chinese infants since life began on the banks of the Yellow River.

Just how willing we are to ignore the issues involved here is shown by a report in *The Irish Times* on 7 March 2008, heralding the opening of Glanbia's new 'human vitamin and minerals plant' in Shanghai, to provide 'the chip inside' infant formula:

'With 18 million babies born there (*in China*) each year – more than Europe, North America and South America combined – it is little surprise that dairy companies have their eyes fixed on China for future profit nourishment, and are investing accordingly,' trumpets the report, which goes on to tell of the Kerry Group's 'double digit growth' in the Asia-Pacific region, while Dairygold Food Ingredients' sales to China had increased by 50 per cent in 2007.

The commercial director of Dairygold Food Ingredients, Aidan Fitzsimons, is quoted as saying that the Asian market is his 'prime target' and the article continues:

> Fitzsimons believes that China's one-child policy, rather than limiting sales, is actually creating demand for 'premium quality, highly functional baby foods' and helping the market there grow by 20 per cent a year. The 'little emperor syndrome,' means that each child is likely to have two parents and four grandparents lavishing attention on his or her welfare and with diets across all ages fast becoming more westernised, that welfare emphatically includes infant milk formula.
>
> In China, people who didn't breastfeed were using cow's milk, which is not appropriate. When formula became available, it was almost seen as a sign of a new world,' says Michael Barry, director of the Irish Dairy Industries' Association (IDIA), a group affiliated to employers' body IBEC.

In a pathetic effort at 'balance', there is a side panel on the 'alleged' misdeeds of Nestlé in the marketing of its formula in developing countries. Gabrielle Palmer believes the formula companies have almost all broken the international code on the marketing of breastmilk substitutes – Nestlé just happened to be the biggest company and was targeted in order make the boycott more effective.

As recently as 2004, Nutricia, which uses Irish milk, was caught by pressure group Baby Milk Action planning to give away 100,000 colourful CDs of popular songs in China with every tin of 'Kissing my Baby' infant formula. The international code explicitly forbids the use of free gifts.

It would be very simple to call for an end to the export of Irish infant formula to developing countries but even if it happened – which it never would – it would just give a bigger market share to someone else. The truth is that the control of the sale of formula must be achieved by adherence to the international code, policed and enforced by national governments.

It's hard to see what a country which is used to central control would lose by a ban on the sale of infant formula. Except, of course, that the international companies – Glanbia included – are now investing in setting up factories in China itself. Selling breastmilk substitutes is always about creating a market for something for which there should be none. It will always result in sub-optimal nutrition for infants and in developing countries it will always endanger the lives of many babies.

# 9

## Coffee Mornings

*'The fact is that women at home are working.'*
Action created by one group of women in the
Report of the National Women's Councils
*Women and Work* Millennium Project, 2000

The way you routinely managed a feature when I worked for *The Irish Times* was that you got a topic, then you got three voices on it. The three voices had to be seen to come from different areas of the topic and often that meant different areas of the country: Killineys were balanced by Darndales, other Killineys were balanced by west Limericks, or, for convenience sake, Corks. Depending on your subject you got an age-range and, of course, a range of opinions. That is how most journalism in this country still works. You're looking for 'balance'.

Of course it is never anything of the kind. You have arbitrarily chosen the three areas of the topic to be covered, for instance: there are lots of others which aren't covered. You may have given balance to a discussion in which all the truth and most of the voices are from one side: for an example of that you need look no further than the inane habit of putting climate change 'sceptics' up against mainstream scientific opinion.

To maintain the illusion of 'balance', you never say how you came by the people to whom you talked. You don't say: here's Mary, she's one of my old schoolfriends, and here's Anna, who's her friend. You act as if you don't know them or even as if they were the first two women who passed on the street in front of the office.

The thing you never do is admit you have chosen them specifically to prove your own argument, although that is exactly what you have nearly always done.

All my instincts for this chapter were to continue these practices, or what Nuala O'Faolain called 'the inherent dishonesty' of journalism. But instead I decided to dump them all.

The interviews I present here are with forty-something, highly qualified professional women, most of whom have given up their jobs, at least temporarily, to give their children more time. They have struggled to do this in different ways, financially or emotionally or both and they have struggled, too, with their wider society.

I was attracted to their stories because they are similar to mine. We are a generation, or more precisely, a subset of a generation. We were immigrants in territory previously unmapped by women, and like immigrants, we have been driven to achieve.

Our definition of achievement has not up to now included raising children. That was the old country.

We thought we were feminists and we probably were but I believe we were in flight from poverty, even if the poverty was never ours.

We wanted children. But we were clear that motherhood would not interfere with our careers. Instead it changed not only how we lived but how we thought.

I think these are amazing interviews. They were not gifts to me from the women who gave them, they were gifts to this debate. The women wanted this story told and took a decision to tell it.

## MARIA DOWLING, 45, PSYCHOTHERAPIST AND MOTHER OF THREE

*Maria Dowling, who lives in north Dublin, gave up her job as a psychotherapist at the Rape Crisis Centre in Dublin two years ago after eleven years. She and I came into contact through a mutual concern for the undervaluation of the work of parenting. I did an interview with the writer Mary Kenny while she was researching an article on feminism today for* Village *magazine. She told me the interview influenced what she wrote. The article concludes: 'The next, most significant phase of feminism, I believe, will be the fight for the right to motherhood, for motherhood to be respected as a choice and for mothers to be entitled to be with their young children and to raise them at home.' (Village,* December 2009–January 2010)

*Maria Dowling, who had formed a discussion group around these issues, emailed Kenny thanking her for her mention of the value of the work of women in the home. Kenny put her in contact with me. During our first phone conversation she said that she was helped by the advice of an older feminist to give up her job because she almost felt she needed 'permission' from the women's movement.*

*One of the factors that prompted her decision to give up her job was when she got some photographs developed and thought her eldest child looked 'sad':*

'I've noticed something happening in the last two years with my eldest son – it's like he came back to life. He was incredibly serious all the time and suddenly he started cracking jokes. I can remember the first time I ever saw him have a belly laugh and that was two years ago. He told me something that had happened at school and we both laughed our heads off. I remember looking at him, thinking, "I've never seen you laugh like that."

'I remember laughing with him and then feeling like a good mum because life had been so serious for me that he couldn't laugh. He couldn't be a kid any more than I could be a kid. There were too many important things to do, it was a question of, "Don't be bothering us," including his father, who was even busier than me.

'He's an awful lot lighter, the child is. I get told an awful lot more.

'My daughter is a sensitive little person and I've been around to help her deal with some crises over the last two years, with her teacher leaving and the death of a child in her class. Something that bothers me, though, is that sometimes I feel she is angry with me. She needs to be more connected to me and I want it too.

The youngest fella always had plenty of me. We call him 'the cuddle stealer'.

'I was snippy yesterday because we have so much to do with getting one of our properties rented and then I could see my eldest fella and he looked anxious. I went into his room early and woke him up, and I said to myself, no, I'm not going to go around like a lunatic trying to get everything done and as I pulled the curtains I realised he'd hopped out of the bed. I turned around and his arms were round my waist and he was hugging me. "Hiya, Mammy. I love you, Mammy."

'I thought…I thought…Sometimes I think you say that because I think you're trying to get on my right side because you're anxious. He picks up on my stress. So I ruffled his hair and I said, "Do you know what, you'd a grumpy Mammy yesterday. What a grouch. I'm so sorry." I walked out of the room and I actually realised that how I am has the power to determine whether or not he will have a good day. I felt his vulnerability as a child and the power I hold regarding impact on any of my kids.'

*She confided in an older feminist, also a therapist:*
'I told her that I thought the children needed more of me than that they're squeaky clean and their grades are all right. I told her I longed to just sit in a field and have them run around me. I think it evoked something in her. She brought me in a tape of an ABBA song, "Slipping through My Fingers". It's about losing your daughter:

> *What happened to the wonderful adventures*
> *The places I had planned for us to go?*
> *Slipping through my fingers all the time*
> *Well, some of that we did but most we didn't*
> *And why I just don't know.*

'I listened to it and I was *inconsolable*. I said to her, "Now, I'm going to give you that back."

"'Oh, you're giving it back to me," she said.

'I said, "'I can't listen to that because that's what I'm doing right now."

'She said, "That's what I did.' She said, "I know I have achieved a lot in this work. I've done most of what people want to do in this field." She could see that I admired her greatly and wanted a legacy like hers. She had blessed so many hurting people and, a skilled, seasoned therapist of high regard, had supervised and encouraged those of us coming in to the work, had taught well and written well. She told me, "I would give it all back."

"'For what?"

"'Just to be where you are right now."

'It was a gift. I really think this woman was a gift to me. Because if she hadn't done that I'd have talked my way into staying and I'd have lost the next ten years.'

*Maria says she was 'split in two'; a hugely maternal person, keenly aware of what society valued and keenly aware of economic realities.*

'I would have had more than three children. When Paul was born – my youngest – I remember saying to my husband, 'We've just enough time for a fourth. But I nearly lost Paul at twenty-seven weeks and my body was older and I wasn't able for more babies.

'I think I've always wanted them very badly but I am only in touch with this at night when they are asleep. I often stand over them at night, looking at them. It's in that silence that I really feel how precious they are to me and how much I want them, want to connect with them, want to be a good mother to them. It's also when I feel any regrets about the day and I resolve to make the next day different.

'I think I want the time now to be different but I'm up against something that's around me that's quite unseemly that tells me it's not valuable.'

*She feels she grew up in a culture in which there was 'indifference' and 'resentment' towards children.*
'Children were seen and not heard and were not really listened to until their late teens. Looking back now, it was "in the air" that this was a generation in which women had little say in how many pregnancies they had.

'My mother was aware of this culture regarding children and felt it deeply. She felt at odds with her own generation and the generation of her own mother regarding the value of children, because my mother was so maternal and just adored children. My mother deeply wanted us but had to contend with the attitudes of her day towards children and it was difficult for her. She didn't have the power as a woman to determine how we were treated by others, in any context, even school. It hurt her and she was troubled for us.'

*Maria was reminded of this attitude when she had her first child. She recalled when an older visitor to her house responded to her baby crying by putting the baby into his pram, throwing a blanket over him, wheeling the pram into a room and closing the door.*
*'Listen to me,' she told Maria, who was trying to get past her to the crying baby. 'Your husband needs his social life back.'*
*Irish society did not teach her to value children.*
'You could rear yourself. If you've got food and clean clothes… The rest was American nonsense. We had an aunt who was a principal of a school in America and she came home to Ireland every year. I could sense that she knew she was in a very different culture in Ireland where kids were concerned. When she talked about the American kids, I recall that the response from listeners was that Americans were "so over the top about their kids". But what did they do that was so over-the-top? They did birthday parties and they listened to them.'

'I loved my aunt's visits. She asked us questions and listened to us like we were adults.'

*Like her mother and aunt, Maria says she has always loved kids.*
I was holding and minding other people's babies all my life. I did a master's degree in America and I paid for it by minding people's babies. I had this incredible maternal…I used to think it went too far with me with the maternal thing and that's why I could never go away with Karl (*her husband*) for a weekend. I couldn't leave them. I was *glad* they couldn't take a bottle.'

*She took parental leave when her third child was born and when she went back to work she says she felt 'a bit of a fraud'.*
'I lasted a year and Karl said, "We're set up – go." At that point I was craving my children. And I thought I'd be running through fields with them. I'd be baking bread. But the minute I came home I thought, "What have I done? Who am I now? I'm nobody. But weren't you a therapist? I felt like I'd lost half of myself."

*She says she can sometimes feel the criticism of her choice in the air when she's having coffee with other women.*
'It's like, "'What's wrong with you?" I just say, "I'm in private practice," and that makes them back off. But if it were to dwindle to nothing…? I'll say what I am. I'm putting three human beings into the world as balanced human beings who will be productive in their own right and in their own way.'

*She understands, however, that she has internalised society's under-valuation of that work. A clear articulation of this struggle comes in a later email:*
'My experience of the six months after I left my job, before I started private practice, was one of feeling that I was like someone unemployed, not contributing to society and indeed making a decision not to contribute. The pressure on educated, professional women is immense. Why are you letting your education be wasted? What a pity. Don't you feel unfulfilled? All that studying and what, you're cleaning a house and doing school runs? There was also a sense that a mother could only tolerate this life of domesticity if she had paid work as an escape on the side.

For me, it seems there is no place of rest, no place to be where I am not tormented. I am damned internally with guilt if I work, because I know I am not there for my children. And I am damned if I don't work.

I am in a battle to find my place of peace and searching for this has been my focus over the last two years. I haven't found it yet but I am more and more aware of the forces around me and I want to fight for what I believe is right. I won't be able to reclaim lost years with my children but I will be able to reclaim a career later on. It disturbs me that I fall into thinking that domestic and mothering work is not valuable. I feel this needs to be spoken about. Women need to write down what they do in a day and imagine the consequences of not doing it. Would it be valued then?

I actively tell myself to stay focused. I tell myself that I am producing the next generation who will relate, work, love and contribute to this society. I am making a contribution. The strongest grounding thought of all, though, is the one when I picture myself as a very old woman, reflecting on life. What will I regret? I want to be able to say I was there for my kids; I loved them well and made the most of the time we were under one roof. I don't want to lament time gone by and opportunities missed. This is heartbreak for me. That Abba song line, "Slipping through my fingers all the time…" would be unbearable.'

*The value Maria places on career is not surprising, given the struggle she had to get her education. She remembers going off on her own to study in corners of the house. She also admits she fears poverty:*
'I think I always had a fear of not having money and a fear of being poor. Not that being hungry or not having things is so bad. It's about shame. When I look back I think I was prepared to compromise motherhood out of shame.'

*Coming back to the interview, she is less hard on herself. She was, she says, motivated to make money to give her children a better life.*
When my husband and I started having babies ten years ago, the

boom was on and Karl and I decided to make the most of it. We were both in well-paying jobs and wanted to make the most of the opportunities open to us. We knew the value of opportunities because we were 1980s college graduates. We knew that opportunities last just a short time and that would be it for us, probably for the rest of our working lives. Hard times growing up had taught us to grab opportunities and make the most of them. We had both experienced people close to us who had done this and some who had not. We decided the boom was our time to do something that would have an impact on our future and the futures of our children.'

*The couple made a series of property investments, beginning with a house bought off the plans in a new estate with no sense of community. Getting out of there and into a good house back in their north Dublin community did not come cheap.*
'Both my husband and myself worked incredibly hard during the Celtic Tiger years. It was not a time for enjoyment. I was exhausted all the time. I told you I got the "green light" from my husband to leave my job two years ago. I was ready to go. I loved my job but the reality is that mothering and therapy work come from the same pot of resources. What is given to clients is not available for children. It's as simple as that.'

*Karl took redundancy and started a business but the economic downturn has been a challenge. Maria is keeping her registration as a therapist and taking clients privately.*
'The dilemma now is how much should I work? I think for me the juggling of a career and motherhood is enormously difficult. My experience of it is one of being pulled in different directions. I love my work and I see how it could sweep me away so easily. I have to keep an eye on how much I do. My sense of motherhood is that it is something into which I want to sink and savour. My maternal inclination is to let myself be swept away by all it brings, where watching a child, noticing their needs and planning and engaging them to meet the needs is what I am about. But this

is not something I am free to be for my children and I probably never will be. There is a hierarchy of needs that I attend to for my children.'

*She makes a key point:*
'For women to reclaim motherhood it has to be safe. The woman, the mother, has to be respected and not rendered vulnerable to being abused, demeaned, devalued for the role she assumes. I am very aware that in this country we are not there yet. Motherhood is not valued. It is actively devalued. Yet there are so many noises made about the value of children and children's development and the need for parents to have good relationships with children. The pulling in different directions that I experience is directly and indirectly an experience of massive contradictions about motherhood's value in our society. I wanted to be at home but it evokes fear in me. I feel vulnerable to the economic consequences of giving up a professional career. But I know is it more. I feel vulnerable to a society that will not support me being in that role and in fact will label me as indulgent, spoilt, not doing something productive and indeed, lazy. If a woman with children were to list what she does all day and call it work, it would be deemed a hard day's labour. What seems to happen though, is that the woman's domestic and maternal work is not counted as work. Consequently, stay-at-home mothers themselves don't see it and count it as work. It's as if this work is invisible.'

## RÓISÍN MURPHY, 43, ARCHITECT AND MOTHER OF THREE

*Róisín Murphy is a well-known architect and – with her trademark flowing curls – TV front woman. She was Senior Design Director at Douglas Wallace when they put the new Brown Thomas in the old Switzers. She became well-known to TV audiences as one of the faces of* Beyond the Hall Door *and* House-hunters in the Sun.
*She is a friend of a friend and she did small but perfectly-formed jobs on my first house and the house I moved into when I married. When we were expecting our fourth child she designed a series of*

*storage units which are still with us. She had her first child around then and we began to have a conversation about her distress at leaving him in the local crèche. She remembers me telling her that her distress was quite natural and recommending getting a child minder. She did this but it still didn't work out for Róisín, because she wanted to be with the child herself.*

*We began to have long discussions about what motherhood was all about. I will never forget her saying, 'Women have the boobs.'*

*In the end, Róisín gave up working in the practice she set up with her partner Dave Purdue and he went out to work. The tale had an all-too-common twist last Christmas when Dave lost his job. Now Róisín is gearing up again to work in her own practice, Warren Architecture and Interiors.*

'If it's going to work, it has to be remote from me,' she says. 'Because I have to have time with the kids and cook dinners and have a life. I do the design work; it's handed over. When I was young I thought it was all about me but it's not, it's about design. I don't have to be in a black suit. I can still do it in my pinny in the back room.'

*Róisín had absolutely no idea that having a child would change her life.*
'I talked Dave into having kids. I said, "You won't notice this child. There's a crèche on the road. It's just one child." But I think that was the end of me, really. It did change everything. I think it's just a bonding thing. If I had to be away from Jay for a couple of hours I got distressed. I would see the girls walking in the street in their jim-jams and I thought, 'They're right.' Life is just about our kids and our family and you have to have that sorted first. It's not about making and spending money. I lost the interest. I wanted to paint. I found myself talking to different people. I was alone a lot.'

*She had another boy and then a little girl.*
'I really, really enjoyed having a family. I just thought this was the business. I didn't want to leave them with anyone else. To hell with

it! We were getting lots of offers of work, but I said to Dave, "Is there any way you can get a job outside the house?'"

*She admits, however, that when she finally gave up work she was 'ashamed':*
'There is an appalling divide between women. If you decide to go to work that's your best sense of what you can do as a mother. Equally if you decide to stay at home...But people find the decision to stay at home hard to understand.

'My family thought it was *appalling* that I wanted to give up work and have kids. I realised that academic achievement was not the pinnacle but in the past you had to have it or you went out of the country with a shovel. We're such a young country. We were a very poor country and it's not long since we came from that. We were so bound by shame and the church and the neighbours. Ann Lovett would rather have killed herself than to have brought shame on her family.'

*She describes her mother as having been "hungry" for education. But she rejects what she calls 'the idea that you are giving away your education by raising kids'.*
You're pouring it into them. My education has changed my kids' life.'

*For her, she says*, 'It wasn't a big deal to give up work. I have to say I think it's nature. I sound like a neanderthal, but I really wanted to look after the kids. But the recession has been really tough on men. Dave has to be busy. It's the busyness that men need.

*Then she says*, 'We are missing one fundamental truth. There is fathering as well as mothering.'

*Dave has come in for a coffee and says*, 'We can't nurture as well.'

'But they have a deeper voice and they don't cry as easily. I can see it's terribly important to boys of a particular age. I think they like to go out and be men.'

*She admits, however, that she had a lot of work to do on herself before she could parent well:* 'We're all products of Ireland in our own way. There was religion, fear of religion, large-scale child-abuse. I didn't want to bring that into the next generation.'

*She describes her kids as:* "free – it's like they've gone to America, psychologically".


*Róisín has been engaged in doing an art project, a series of water-colours of north Dublin buildings in which institutional abuse went on. When she came to the city from Kildare to study architecture at Bolton Street College of Technology, she boarded above a Magdalen Laundry in Henrietta Street, which she has since painted.*

'I found that harrowing. That young girls and young women were almost bred out of us. Did Irish people as a nation pick good-looking women and say, "We're going to get rid of them?" If a girl was too flirtatious, she was sent off. People were so frightened of it. Can we ever reclaim that?'


*Active as a student against the destruction of Dublin, Róisín is now more interested in the city's social fabric:*

'Then it was about saving the city physically. Now it's about saving it spiritually.'


*Like many stay-at-home parents, she has become very involved in her local community: she was involved in rehousing her local school and is working with an 'urbanist' friend to try to foster communities in the city. Reading Constantia Maxwell's* Dublin under the Georges *during the Celtic Tiger era had a huge impact – the excess of the years before the Act of Union were followed by total collapse.*

'I got very spooked. I thought, this is what's going to happen. I got a real ominous sense around 2001.'


*She remembers with horror that when she was designing the new Brown Thomas she didn't want to use their old Waterford glass chandeliers:*

'*Waterford glass chandeliers!* But Hilary Weston (the wife of the

Canadian owner) knew. She said, "'You're taking them. Get over it.'" I was so nouveau riche, I couldn't respect it. I actually think we were going to put blue blobby glass on them! And when I think Waterford Glass has gone out of business, a company *driven* by quality.'

*Now, she says*: 'I'm behaving more like my mother. She was a farmer's daughter from the west of Ireland and you keep things. You patch things. Life is very short and very painful if you spend *all* your time trying to get money.'

## ORLA BOURKE, 47, BROADCASTER AND MOTHER-OF-FOUR, MEABH SMITH, 45, ENGINEER AND MOTHER-OF-THREE

*Orla Bourke found my number in the phone book and rang me up out of the blue a couple of years ago. She had read some articles on mothers and children I had written in* The Irish Times. *Her friend Meabh Smith had written a manual for women who want to take time out of the workforce to raise children and she wondered if I could make suggestions on how to get it into the public domain.*

*I met the two women in Dublin's Gresham Hotel and we had a fantastic conversation. I came away with the conviction that I should go back to my idea of writing a book on motherhood in Ireland but that I should try to bring in these women as co-authors. Meanwhile Meabh Smith decided to go the way of the web and set up her own website to tackle the issues facing mothers today: www. mummy.ie*

*We regrouped in the Gresham for another conversation, but this time I taped it. Says Orla:*
'I would have been your archetypal feminist. I went to Trinity. I did well. I kept my own surname when I got married.

I had my first child, Dearbhla, when I was working as a staff journalist with the *Sunday Press*. When the *Press* closed, I went to RTÉ as a radio news reporter. I had a second child, a boy, Daire, three years later.

I managed to breastfeed both children and continue working. However things started changing because the jobs I took had to fit in with them. I wasn't unleashed and free. I didn't realise it then but I am actually a very competitive person. My mother was the only woman on our road to go back to work after the youngest went to school.

*Orla worked in many capacities in RTÉ. She was a researcher on the* Liveline *phone-in radio show and she produced a raft of different feature programmes. She had her first child at thirty, her second at thirty-three.*
'All my colleagues who weren't having babies were shooting up in their careers and I was still staying at the same level. I had a home birth with my second baby and that was a really positive experience for me. I had this wonderful midwife, Kate Spillane. I became conflicted. I felt I had to have a third child even though I knew it would force a change in the direction of my career.

'I did feel trapped by my decision at times. I loved my work in RTÉ but the hours demanded by many jobs there simply didn't fit in with rearing children in a way I wanted. There were very few role models for me then.'

*She remembers a comment someone in RTÉ made, approvingly, about 'successful' women there: 'They'd eat babies for breakfast.'*
'And that was something to be proud of!'

*After her fourth child, Grainne, was born, Orla had to change her career track and took leave from RTÉ. She emails later to ask me to mention the importance of the support of her husband Ken in all her decisions.*
*Again, she had the baby at home and she describes it as 'an incredible experience'.*
'It's a psychosexual thing, having a baby. We've become so detached. There's obstetrics and this complete disconnect with ourselves as women. When I was in labour with Grainne I tapped into a creative part of myself that I'd never tapped into before. And I believe this will feed into any future work I might do in a totally positive way.'

*Orla has thought a lot about the psychological effect of breastfeeding on women. Is it significant that the generation of second-wave feminism, which came before us, often didn't breastfeed, she wonders? As we have seen, Friedan's* The Feminine Mystique *coincided with the collapse of breastfeeding in the US and the reduction of motherhood to how many things you can buy to make your house nice for your husband.*

*Since she has been on leave Orla has been working on a creative project at home. She says this is 'something for the future' and if she manages to bring it to fruition, it will all have been worth it. She gets to be there for her children but also, hopefully, can put her years of education to good use. Because otherwise, she asks:*
How else can we fit work in with kids? The whole education/ workplace system has to change to facilitate not just the male timeline but the female rhythm, which is very different.'

*Meabh, who works part-time as Senior Clinical Engineer at Beaumont Hospital after spending five years out of the workforce, comes in on this point:*
'There's a whole focus on equality for women in education…but the reality is the day you become a mother you will slow down your progress. It doesn't matter if you stay full-time or part-time or you give up. The children at second level see women who seem to juggle it all successfully but they don't realise the cost. There is no debate and no discussion so how can there be change? Because they are the people who can bring change.'

*Orla:* 'We need to be truthful about what it's like. People are lying through their teeth. I hated leaving my child in a crèche. And I'd be leaving the house every day in my suit and briefcase because everyone told me that was what you did. "You're educated, you've a right. Don't be such a wuz." I'd be skiving off work early to get to her. My instinct was telling me – you want to be with that baby. A child needs its mother. It needs to be breast-fed. It needs that bond. And the mother needs it too.'

*She says part of the problem is that so many feminist texts were written by women who'd yet to have children or had chosen not to have them at all.*
'I use to think like that too. You don't always get it until you've had kids. It's like a switch that gets flipped on.'
*Meabh:* 'I definitely didn't get it.'

*Meabh's mother qualified as a nurse but never practised. She stayed home to rear seven of them in rural Northern Ireland. She would not have had it any other way, Meabh thinks, except that she had no money of her own.*
'She was shocked and horrified when I took a five-year career break. She couldn't believe the concept that you'd have money and you'd give it up.'

*Meabh worked half-time from the birth of her first child and had a child minder at home.*
'My sister arrived at the house one day to find the child minder drunk. So I quit work. I didn't work after that for another five-and-a-half years.'

*She is back working twenty hours a week but she is replacing someone who worked full-time at the same job.*
'I tend to get up early on Saturday and Sunday mornings and work. I love my job but the only way I can do it is to do hours outside work. I don't mind that, except that I'm afraid of losing my humanity. Friends – these people it was easy to make time for and they made time for you. But the juggling will get easier as the kids get older. The goal is to be role model, but not a slave – to home or to work. I would love to have time for humanity and to contribute to the world as well.

*Meabh says she took 'an engineer's approach' to being at home with the children when she was off, read the books and thought it through. She is currently researching what is the best balance for the family.*

'I have thought a lot about it. I can do the cooking and shopping and cleaning. What I need is someone to be there just for me. To pick me up. That I can fall apart in front of. Men, to a large extent, have lost that role. And we pushed them into it. That they have to do half the hoovering etc…'

*Meabh's adolescence, like Orla's was dominated by an emphasis on education:*
'As Catholics in the North, we put a huge emphasis on educating yourself out of the North.'

*Although at university she went into the predominantly male area of engineering:*
'I did not come across bias. I did not see the need to be a feminist. But I have become a feminist. Because I now understand what it's about. It's about the right to be a mother. For me, that's what it's about. Ann Crittenden has that famous comment that recognition for motherhood is "the great unfinished business of the women's movement."'

# 10

## FIVE MOTHERS IN CLONTARF

*Margaret is a friend of Maria Dowling. Interested in this project because of her own experience of becoming a mother, she organised a meeting in her house in Clontarf, on the northside of Dublin, and I taped it. Five mothers aged between forty-five and fifty from different corners of this country and beyond sat down that day to coffee and polenta cake and had one of the most open discussions of motherhood in Ireland that I have ever heard. The women asked me to change their names because of the frankness of the exchange.*

*The conversation focused a lot on fertility difficulties, which all the women had experienced to very different degrees.*

*Barbara had a fertility issue made worse by the fact that she started trying for a baby in her late thirties. This is something she could not say at the time but she can say it now. She describes having her children as 'a long and difficult journey'.*

'For me, infertility was the most difficult grief because it's so unacknowledged. If you have a parent who's died, if you have a child who's died – people can very legitimately say, "I'm so sorry," and that carries you but you can't go into work and say, "I've just discovered I'm infertile." My consultant, who became a very good friend, described it as a "chronic grief".

'I remember that exact moment when she said to me that I would have great difficulties conceiving. I was devastated. When I went home I took out a page and I wrote down what age my mother was when she had me and I calculated what age my grandmother was when she had my mother. Trying to find out this family tree through maternal lines. And saying, it stops here.

'One of the things that really struck me was…how I felt lied to. Very powerfully lied to. By the culture of *Cosmopolitan* and *New Woman*. Even though I would never have thought I would be influenced like that because I had a very strong culture, very strong family, very strong faith. There was that feminist thing.

'I remember contacting single friends who I thought were being foolish with their precious time and without telling them my own tragedy, saying, "If you want a child, you may not have all the time you think you have."'

*Barbara, from Kerry, met her husband when she was twenty-one and decided straight away that she was going to marry him. But knowing they were too young, she 'pushed him away' and they both had other relationships, which they 'sabotaged' to end up together. Meanwhile, after a B.Comm in University College, Dublin, Barbara had a series of high-powered careers. She ran a recruitment consultancy in the UK, then, having got a US visa under one of the lottery schemes for Irish citizens, she went there, studied medical insurance and did a law diploma. She thinks the focus on career can be traced back to her education.*

'I went to a convent school. The nuns were the most liberated people who were in the school, in many ways. It was all careers. A lot of them were made principals by the time they were thirty. It was all career and status but also changing the world and bringing God's love to bear on the world. Career and faith: it was a particular brand of feminism.'

*Angela, from Galway, first a nurse and later a lecturer in nursing, says she comes from a similar background to that of her friend, Barbara.*

'In our school there were the girls who would go for careers and as for the girls who weren't into education, it was, "You'll be the mothers."'

'That wasn't what I would have learned at home. My mother didn't marry till she was in her thirties and she had eight children. What she wanted for us was that being in a relationship was not the only defining way to live your life. To be self-sufficient as a woman was very important. I delivered my first child when I was twenty-one and I rang my mother and said it was the most powerful thing. She said having children was one of the most important things she'd ever done in her life but you have to be ready for it.'

*This influenced Angela, who had her two children, after some delay, in her late thirties:*
'My husband and I moved a lot. We had a busy life. We said if we didn't have children it wouldn't be the end of our world. But I think no one understands the meaning of not having children until they face it. When people make decisions about having children or not having children early in their lives, I don't think they're fully informed decisions. I don't think we appreciate the biological clock. It goes back to our education.'

*In which motherhood wasn't mentioned?*
'Oh, absolutely not. But I say to the young women I know, "Don't ever presume on your fertility." I think it comes down to this cultural perception that we're in control. Our generation was led to believe that we had control. But the very important things in life we have no control over. We have difficulty accepting things. It was, "I'm ready now. I'll have the baby now."'

*Carmel, from Limerick, is a friend and nursing colleague of Anne's, working in education:*
*Carmel*: 'But if you're not ready...It's not right to have a baby when you're not ready. Girls I went to school with, I knew their potential and they never realised it...'
*Angela*: 'But is potential measured by what you achieve in your career?'
*Carmel*: 'I should have said, "career potential".'
*Angela*: 'Motherhood changed my whole attitude to work – so incredibly. I thought I knew but I didn't know. When young women in the family ask me, I say, "Try to get whatever you want to do careerwise *done* before you become a mother." Because for

me combining work and motherhood has been the most difficult thing of all. I completed my master's when my second child was four months old. He was a great baby. But I would say to them, "Don't do that." I would personally have preferred not to have had that pressure on me. You don't know until you're there how difficult it is to leave your children.

'There was a woman doing a master's in career guidance in my university and I said to her, "Talk about careers that are compatible with motherhood."

*Carmel*: But I went to school in west Limerick with girls who got eight or nine As in the Leaving Certificate and the only thing question they were asked was: "Did you get the call?"'

*Barbara*: 'It was known as the *glaoch*.'

*Carmel*: 'The "call" to primary teacher training in Mary I (Mary Immaculate College, Limerick). Yes, the nuns were into career but it was limited. The girls were looked on as future mothers and they wanted them to go into teaching because they would be off every summer. The ultimate goal was the "call". Now I would reflect on that.'

*Barbara*: 'I'm researching suitable jobs to combine with mother-hood. I was running a programme for children who have just been diagnosed with a disability and I was changing my second fella, thinking, how would I get more speech therapy for a certain child…And I realised I wasn't present to my own child.

'But suitable jobs exist. I know a woman who is a pilot. She parks the plane and off you go.'

*Angela*: 'What happens if she's doing the transatlantic route? How you juggle work and motherhood is an acting role. There is a charade going on.

'I stayed at home for five-and-a-half years and I absolutely loved it. Because I felt I best understood my children. I didn't want anyone else to mind them. I used to be away from them for twelve hours at a time. Seeing them every three hours…that actually matters to me.'

*Carmel*: 'I'm delighted we have these dilemmas.'

*Margaret, from the midlands, remembers working as a nurse in the US, heavily pregnant and with severe pre-eclampsia, with 'stars falling in front of my eyes'. With only six weeks' unpaid maternity leave, she had to give up her job. But she found the 'paradigm shift' traumatic:*

Margaret: 'I was *sobbing*. It was soul-destroying. I remember saying to friends, "Why didn't you tell me it would be like this?" and they said, "It wouldn't have made any difference."'

*Since she came back to Ireland, she combines studying for a degree with caring for her child.*

'But in Ireland, work is the key. You're put in a box. When people ask me what do you work at, I say I'm a kept woman. That response silences them. As someone said to me, "You're a feminist now only in theory, not in practice."

'What has to happen is respect. Respect for the choices people have made and for those who have no choice. To value the women (or men) who stay at home or work outside the home. You should be valued for you, not what you do.'

*Carmel says she would not have been ready for children before she had them, in her thirties, although she did have a series of miscarriages, which are more common the older you are. I spoke to her after the scanning scandal, which had the effect of leaving many woman who had a D and C after one scan wondering if their baby had been alive.*

Carmel: 'I was encouraged strongly to have D and Cs and I had them. The last few days in the media are not doing me any good. I'm numb. I don't want to go there with myself. I'm locking it out.'

Angela: 'I think routine D and Cs comes down to the desire of the hospital for control. Miscarriage is unclear, unrecognised, messy. It's not clear-cut and that's women.'

Barbara: 'We're over-critical of our country. We have a very, very good infant mortality rate and that is a massive achievement.'

Carmel: 'I think there is a strong influence of religion in that. Once they're born, we have to keep babies alive no matter what and it is more the influence of religion than for their wellbeing or our wellbeing as a nation.'

*Angela*: 'I remember working in a Catholic hospital in Australia. We were aborting on one side of the hospital and if the child took a breath it was taken over to the neonatal intensive care unit. Some of those children did live. But what was their quality of life?'

*Sarah (A friend from the US)*: 'Can you have amniocentesis in Ireland?'

Several women: 'Yes.'

*Sarah*: 'And if there's a problem what happens then?'

*Carmel*: 'It's still a grey area.'

*Angela*: 'I wouldn't like amniocentesis to be routine. In the UK I had to sign that I didn't want an amnio.'

*Barbara says she has a Down's Syndrome child among her close relatives.*

*Barbara*: 'The worst thing is not the disability. It's society's pity. You can't control life.

'I remember when I had my first child…I was forty. She was stillborn. As I carried her coffin I was saying, "Thank you, Aoife, for making me a mother."'

*When she can talk, she says,* 'Faith did equip me with tools. I realised it wasn't God who caused this, it was random. But God is in the response. There was the love and support we got from the consultant to the nurses.'

*Angela*: 'There is a power in the gift of motherhood.'

*Barbara*: 'There is the power of becoming a mother.'

## 11

## Feminism Could Still Change the World

*When she greets her friends, I am aware*
*mothercraft has blinded her, till anxiety*
*thins her voice, I want to call out,*
*that for her, now is filled*
*with simple certainties – a spilled cup,*
*a rowdy room, a bed-time story. But*
*as she moves down the street, I can*
*only guess the weight*
*of her sacrifice, her tenderness*
*as her hands keep emptying, emptying…*
'A Young Woman with a Child in Each Hand, Angela
Greene, *Silence and the Blue Night*, Salmon Publishing,
(1993)

When Tom was five years old the state psychological services attributed his developmental difficulties, in part, to my 'traditional role in the home'.

'Traditional role?' I spluttered.

'Don't be offended,' said the social worker. 'Fifty per cent of Irishwomen are *still* in the home.'

'I'm not offended,' I said. 'I just differ from you philosophically.'

I think this was the moment of this book's conception. Readers will differ as to whether or not it has a right to life but I found I could not live with myself if I kept silent.

This outburst from the social worker had been building for some time. Interestingly, the psychological services regarded me as the problem from the beginning: the mother is always the problem; all that has changed is the reason why. For the state psychological service in 2005, my problem was that I did not 'work'.

The service was also hampered by a psychological technique that might be regarded as post-Freudian and consisted in believing that whatever the client said, he or she meant the opposite. As can be imagined, this made communication difficult.

'I gave up my job because I wanted to give up my job.'

'You were too busy to continue in your job.'

It went on and on. I remember the moment when I felt I made something of a breakthrough. I was asked for the hundredth time if I found it stressful having the children at home during their summer holidays and I said, 'No, I love having them at home.' The new social worker – the holder of the poker-hot 'traditional role' theory had disappeared – said that for the first time he understood that I might enjoy my children.

What a mad idea!

What did they know? Most of the time I was dealing with young social workers who did not have children themselves. What kind of society would send a forty-something mother-of-four to a twenty-something without children *for advice*?

The time that was spent by state services attempting to dissuade me from rearing my children was time which was desperately needed by other people. The three other children who were being reared in my home had no negative behavioural symptoms but they were never even given the once-over by the services.

What was wrong with my child was that he was autistic. But when I said I felt his behaviour was abnormal and did not originate in family problems, the response was, and I quote: 'So now you're blaming him, are you?'

I now have superb services for Tom and I am deeply grateful for them. Listening to all that nonsense from the social workers did me no harm except that it wasted my time. I feel outrage for a different mother: a younger, poorer, less well-educated woman than myself. Imagine that she thinks she's doing her best for her difficult child by staying at home to rear him! Imagine she's told she's failing him by not going out to work!

The 43.1 per cent of Irish mothers who are at home full-time are regarded as second-class citizens. The 24.8 per cent of Irish mothers who are working part-time are regarded as a percentage of first-class citizens. The kind of psychological damage that this is doing to women can only be guessed at.

'For women to reclaim motherhood it has to be safe,' as mother-of-three and psychotherapist Maria Dowling says in her interview in Chapter 9. 'The woman, the mother, has to be respected and not rendered vulnerable to being abused, demeaned and devalued for the role she assumes.' (see page 161) I remember the leaflet on postnatal depression I was given in the National Maternity Hospital which identified poverty and social isolation as risk factors. No kidding, I thought. Hormones must play their part but so do social factors. And I am sure that the undervaluation of motherhood by this society must contribute to the incidence of post-natal depression.

In the words of Penelope Leach:

> Males, particularly medical males, like to refer to all postnatal depression as 'hormonal' – part of the myth of menstrual moon-madness men use to excuse themselves the effort of understanding why women weep. Of course there is much hormonal activity in the bodies of newly delivered women. But in more child-orientated societies 'baby blues' are so rare that the very concept is hard to communicate, as this puzzled west-African response shows: 'Has this unhappy woman you tell me of not got her child?'

On 26 May 2010 *The Irish Times* published a supplement called 'Sisters' to celebrate 'Forty years of change in the lives of women'. It included a file entitled 'Agents of Change: Twenty-five Women Who Made a Difference'.

As I read through it, I became aware that the list explicitly excluded any 'difference' made by any woman through her role as a mother, although that is precisely the way in which most women on the planet make the biggest 'difference'.

Mamo McDonald of the Irish Countrywomen's Association is described as having made a difference almost *despite* her eleven children.

You could argue that the 'difference' being discussed here was that made by 'agents of change' in the Irish women's movement over the past forty years. But this argument meant nothing to me that day because it was the same day my son Tom turned around to me suddenly and said, 'Why do you have to help me with my homework when the others can do theirs on their own?'

I remember turning to the sink, seething with rage, and thinking, 'Can helping Tom with his homework not be described as "making a difference"?'

The editorial which accompanied the supplement makes the welcome point: 'There is pride in remembering the courage of those who fought for basic equality,' but continues in the well-worn groove: 'There is also perhaps a degree of dismay and discouragement in reflecting on the reality that legal change has not in itself swept away all of the inequalities. Legislating for equal pay, for example, has only partly closed the gender pay gap: so long as women have to take on a disproportionate commitment to domestic work and childcare, notional equality will not be translated into reality.'

Where in the name of God did we get the idea that the only kind of equality worth having is the same amount of money in our wallets?

Where is the evidence that women take on more 'domestic work and childcare' than men because they 'have to'?

Is there any country in the world in which men and women do even vaguely similar amounts of 'domestic work and childcare'?

How could anyone enforce a regime whereby men and women did equal amounts of 'domestic work and childcare?'

Shouldn't the person who takes on the 'childcare' be the person who's best at it? Isn't that person likely to be the one who wants to do it?

How are we in a situation in which we cannot put any value on the raising of the next generation except to lump it in with 'domestic work' as something which should be shared equally, like household chores?

Are 'domestic work' and 'childcare' equivalent in any way except that they are not paid?

Why is this?

I am aware of the irony in all this. As I write, my husband is away with the children for the weekend so that I can finish this book. It's the first time I've spent a night in my own house without the children since Jack was born eleven years ago.

It feels very odd. It's a sunny bank holiday weekend and I am stuck in front of my computer with only the dog for company. I'm engaged in the classic, western 'me against the odds' exercise in solitary masochism in order to seem exceptional. What am I trying to prove?

I might be better employed spending time with my husband and kids. Without doubt I am writing this book partly to validate my own caring work. I am also writing it because I developed a sense of myself as a writer so early that I can't root it out. Although I am conscious of the conditioning which has meant I need to 'achieve', it's still there.

But to be fair to myself, I really do believe in the value of the caring work of women. I see it being ignored. I want to make it visible. I see the invisibility of this caring work as a symptom of a much wider malaise which makes us ignore anything which isn't bought and sold. That's why breastfeeding doesn't matter and infant formula does. That's why mothers don't matter but childcare services do.

I think an economic system that learned how to value motherhood could change the world. I have found my guru in Marilyn Waring, author of *If Women Counted: a New Feminist Economics*. This classic was first published in 1988 when I was starting out as a journalist but I never remember hearing about it and can't find any references to it in Irish media archives. I got the reference from the Minority Report to the Second Commission on the Status of Women, 1993 by Finola Kennedy: you remember, that right-wing, Catholic mother-of-six 'from the backwoods'?

Marilyn Waring is considered by some bloggers to be New Zealand's only public intellectual. Born in 1952, she became an MP for the National Party at the age of twenty-three but caused a scandal when she threatened to vote with the opposition for a nuclear-free New Zealand. The prime minister called a snap election because of this threat to the government's stability and was demolished at the polls.

Waring has held a string of influential posts, in New Zealand and elsewhere, and is now Professor of Public Policy at the University of Auckland. But my favourite nugget of information about her is the fact that she farmed angora goats until recently, but gave it up at the age of fifty to move to the city.

Childless and an advocate for gay rights, Waring doesn't exactly have the profile Irish commentators expect of a champion of the value of women's work in the home. But this is what she says: 'Every time I see a mother with an infant I know I am seeing a woman at work.'

From another windswept island at the other end of the world, I salute Marilyn Waring. She has made the amazing discovery that economics has a 'statistical conspiracy' to exclude women's work. Throughout the world, she says, women's work is simply not counted: 'There is one unwritten rule: if women do it in an unpaid capacity in their homes, in their garden plots or in the community, it is housework.'

Waring shows how this conspiracy works all over the world. In the developing world, small percentages of women are recorded in censuses as being 'economically active', while in fact they often perform most of the work. It's just a question of what you call work: in Bangladesh, for instance, the census was changed in 1974 to refer to women engaged in unpaid work as 'housewives', whereas before they were described as engaged in 'productive economic activity'.

This is exactly the process which Finola Kennedy, in *Cottage to Crèche*, describes as having happened to the Irish census when it conformed with British standards in 1871. We have never recovered.

Waring also asks the question why it is that the census does not record, as part of the income of the household, the management of that income by a woman in the home. All that squeezing out of the bottom of the toothpaste and shining scuffed shoes and darning socks which people in their forties now remember their mothers doing…it counted for nothing then and it is probably no wonder that most mothers in Ireland do less of it now. Conserving anything became unfashionable because it didn't fuel the growth wanted by what Waring calls the 'patriarchal triumvirate': politicians, economists and statisticians.

It became clear to Waring that conventional economics often reward the destruction of the planet and of human happiness. They concern themselves with the conversion of a natural resource into something which can be traded: cutting down a tree and selling the wood or blasting a quarry, for instance. These activities erode the 'natural capital' of the world, which is regarded as both limitless and worthless. They may also, in certain circumstances, erode the happiness of the world's people, but that, like mother's care and mother's milk, which make people very happy indeed, counts for nothing.

War is growth, remember. Catching and reflecting a baby's first smile is not worth anything.

If our national accounts valued human wellbeing, the world could be a different place. First of all, of course, they would have to understand that 'natural capital' is finite and that its conservation is important.

The Irish emit more carbon per person than any other nation in Europe: 17.5 tonnes, compared with the Swedes, at 7.5 tonnes, for instance. The Chinese are often blamed for our environmental woes but they emit only about 3.5 tonnes per person. The poverty-stricken Malawians emit just 1.8 tonnes.

Stop Climate Chaos say we would need seven planet earths to

supply us with natural resources if all the world lived like the Irish.

Well, we don't have them and we can't get them.

We have to learn to use up fewer of the earth's resources in our daily lives if we are to survive on this planet. The new kind of 'growth' has got to be in human development – which rather calls into question the OECD's description of a woman raising children at home as a waste of human capital. Raising children who are secure, loving and confident is a major contribution to society by any parent and a contribution that will pay dividends, as those children go on to do the same for their own.

Which is not to say, of course, that children who go tragically off the rails don't often come from excellent homes. As I, the mother of a disabled child, know well, we all come into the world with a genetic kit bag. And there are factors in a child's environment which no parent can control.

But a good parent with a difficult child or a child in difficult circumstances will often limit the damage caused to the child and which the child may cause. Even though some parents lose the fight for their children, the fight is still worthwhile.

There's little point just patting parents in the home on the back and saying, 'Don't mind what they say, you *are* making a contribution.' No, you've got to count their work and you've got to reward it.

New systems to replace GDP are being developed because it is clear that we can't stick to an accounting system which makes environmental and social destruction look like progress. In the US, pioneers of what is known as 'steady state economics', Herman Daly and John Cobb, came up with the *Index of Sustainable Economic Welfare* in 1989. In the UK, the New Economics Foundation has developed a series of indices, looking at environmental and social indicators as well as perceptions of happiness, called the Happy Planet Index. (Jonathon Porritt, *Capitalism: As If the World Matters*)

If we used it, we might understand that our happiness does not hinge entirely on how many things we buy and sell. I will never forget a chilling comment which a long-term breast-feeder made in the *Guardian* (30 April 2005) when asked why people found her behaviour objectionable: 'The market doesn't like happy people.'

It's not just that we're running out of natural resources. The planet's ability to deal with our waste is running out too. The spectre of 'runaway climate change' is haunting us. Lee Scott, Chief Executive of Wal-Mart, famously compared our warming climate to 'Hurricane Katrina in slow motion' before setting out to make massive changes in how he runs his business.

Some think we will eventually have a system by which we will all have a carbon allowance and trade our surplus. It's an attractive idea because it would surely be a means of taking from the rich and giving to the poor. It would also be a way of rewarding a parent who stays close to home with a couple of children and perhaps grows a few vegetables. If environmental damage cost the damager, life in the slow lane might be more financially viable. It's a new twist to the conservation which most of our mothers practised in their daily lives, as they tried to keep the clasps of their battered purses closed.

It seems clear that we must think of ways of paying parents for what they do, particularly if we abandon the scramble to get everyone to use as many resources as possible. If resources are limited, we have to redistribute better to those who have less of them if society is not going to break down.

And we have to give parenting a place as a core activity in society.

As we know, the Second Commission on the Status of Women ruled out a payment to the parent in the home on the grounds that it would be 'predominantly a benefit to the earning partner'. Well, we've moved on – most of us. As we have seen, the Commission on the Family recognised the need for a payment to parents and went through some models.

One option is to pay a guaranteed basic income to every man, woman and child to cover their needs. It replaces all benefits and most income tax allowances. There are different versions of this popular idea and Porritt says it is under research in many countries, including Ireland, Holland, New Zealand, Australia, the US, Germany, Sweden, France, Canada and Brazil. But I have always had an instinctive hesitation about basic income as a reward for parents because it doesn't recognise their work.

Child benefit does recognise this work but because it is untaxed, it has no impact on relative poverty. The current government tried to find a way of taxing child benefit before the budget of December 2009 but there is a legal obstacle to doing this because of individualisation.

Not only should carers in the home have taxable income, they should have access to state benefits. People must not be impoverished in their old age because they spent a lot of their time caring for others when they were younger.

But I'm with the Second Commission on the Status of Women on one thing: the household income should be shared equally by both partners, by law.

During 2010 it emerged that a hundred and eighty-eight children who were in contact with, or known to the Health Service Executive died in the previous ten years. Every one of these deaths is a tragedy. But I am beginning to wonder whether the outrage isn't an important distraction from knowledge that we all bear some responsibility for those deaths, just as we are all responsible for the abuse of children by religious and priests. Perhaps we will eventually accept that our whole society has abused children: that, to some extent, we have all both abused children and *been* abused children.

I loved Anne Enright's Man Booker-winning novel, *The Gathering*. Despite the fact that my childhood was free from the horrors of abuse and suicide, I can recognise in it the casual cruelty with which children of my generation were so often treated. 'All our parents were mad in those days,' Enright writes.

There were reasons for this in our complex history, reasons that may also explain the challenge that being a mother has presented to many women of my generation.

Most Irishwomen can now choose how many babies to have and they are having lots of them. According to 2009 figures, our fertility is the highest in the EU: the recession has not dented it. As an indicator of the welfare of young Irish women, these birth statistics say to me loud and clear that they don't fear motherhood as my generation did.

Maybe the Famine is over at last. Maybe the boom did that for us.

I write this as I face the end of my own fertility. I feel the clock slowing down, its rusty cogs turning with more and more difficulty.

I wrote the first chapter of this book only last year; yet already the children it describes are gone. There are no more 'dangerous rides' down the stairs in blankets. The twins no longer 'boing' around the house, shouting, 'We're the bangaroos.'

Walking back from the local river with the four of them yesterday, it struck me suddenly that I am in the last days of the happiest years of my life.

# REFERENCES IN THE TEXT

| | |
|---|---|
| Page 11 | Catherine Hakim, *Key Issues in Women's Work: Female Diversity and the Polarisation of Women's Employment*, p. 207. |
| Pages 13-4 | Elgy Gillespie (ed.). *Changing the Times – Irish Women Journalists, 1969-81*, p. 57. |
| Page 14 | Hakim, *op. ci*t., p. 200. |
| Pages 14-5 | Daphne de Marneffe, *Maternal Desire: Our Children, Love and the Inner Life*, p. 13. |
| Page 15 | *Ibid.*, p. 295. |
| Page 17 | Hakim, *op. cit.*, p. 63. |
| Page 18 | Hakim, *op. cit.*, p. 87. |
| Page 27 | Sue Gerhardt, *Why Love Matters: How Affection Shapes a Baby's Brain*, pp. 43, 64. |
| Page 30 | Melissa Benn, *Madonna and Child: Towards a New Politics of Motherhood*, p. 33. |
| Page 32 | Caitriona Clear, *Women of the House: Women's Household Work in Ireland 1922-61*, p. 11. |
| Page 35 | Hakim, *op. cit.*, p. 78. |
| Pages 38-9 | Commission on the Family, *Strengthening Families for Life*, p. 5.8. |
| Page 43 | Penelope Leach, *Children First*, p. 34. |
| Page 46 | Tim Callan (ed.), *How Unequal? Men and Women in the Irish Labour Market*, p. xxii. |
| Pages 47-8 | *Report of the Second Commission on the Status of Women*, p. 71. |
| Page 49 | *Ibid.*, p. 40. |
| Page 50 | Benn, *op. cit.*, p. 36. |
| Page 50 | *Report of the First Commission on the Status of Women*, p. 204. |
| Page 51 | *Report of the Second Commission on the Status of Women*, p. 78. |
| Page 52 | *Minority Report of the Second Commission on the Status of Women*, pp. 396, 420. |
| Page 54 | Germaine Greer, *The Female Eunuch*, p. 251. |
| Page 55 | National Women's Council's, *An Accessible Childcare Model*, p. 8. |
| Page 56 | Mary Kenny, *Woman x Two: How to Cope with a Double Life*, p. 14 |
| Page 61 | Hakim, *op. ci*t., p. 70. |
| Page 64 | Nuala O'Faolain, *Are You Somebody?*, p. 10. |
| Page 65 | June Levine, *Sisters*, p. 9. |
| Page 65-6 | *Ibid.*, p. 24. |

Page 67        Nuala Fennell, *Irish Marriage: How are You?*, p. 6,
Page 68        Nuala Fennell, *op. cit.*, pp. 81, 15, 81.
Page 69        Nuala Fennell, *A Political Woman*, pp. 42, 45.
Page 69        Betty Friedan, *The Feminine Mystique*, p. 276.
Page 70        Friedan, *op. cit.*, pp. 316, 16, 219, 350.
Page 71        Betty Friedan, *The Second Stage*, p. 10.
Page 76        Hakim, *op. cit.*, p. 14.
Page 79        OECD, *Babies and Bosses*, p. 138.
Page 79        National Economic and Social Forum, *Early Childhood Care
               and Education*, p. 59.
Page 93        Hakim, *op. cit.*, p. 83.
Page 94        Sarah Blaffer Hrdy, *Mother Nature: Maternal Instincts and the
               Shaping of the Species*, p. 275.
Page 95        Ann Crittenden, *The Price of Motherhood: Why the Most
               Important Job in the World Is Still the Least Valued*, p. 7.
Page 96        Joseph Robins, *A Study of Charity Children in Ireland 1700-
               1900*, pp. 16, 30.
Page 97        Robins, *op. cit.*, p 35.
Page 98        *National Children's Strategy*, p. 6.
Page 99        Colin Heywood, *A History of Childhood*, pp. 131, 156.
Page 99        Crittenden, *op. cit.*, pp 49-50.
Page 100       Crittenden, *op. cit.*, p. 51.
Page 101       *National Children's Strategy*, pp. 19, 51.
Page 102       NESF, *Early Childhood and Education*, p. 125.
Page 105       Clear, *op. cit.*, p. 5.
Page 106       Leach, *Children First*, p. 81.
Page 109       *Planning Guidelines*, Dublin, June, 2001, p. 1.1.
Page 110       *Ibid*. p. 2.2.
Page 112       Norman Ruddock, *The Rambling Rector*, quoted in Diarmuid
               Ferriter, *Occasions of Sin: Sex and Society in Modern Ireland*,
               p. 244.
Page 113-4     Mary Kenny, *Goodbye to Catholic Ireland*, p. 228.
Page 114       Heywood, *op. cit.*, p. 79.
Page 116       Fitness to Practice Committee of the Medical Council, 2003.
Page 117       Sheila O'Connor, *Without Consent*, p. 9.
Page 118       *Ibid.*, pp. 289, 264.
Page 119       *Ibid.*, p. 389.
Page 124       Kieran O'Driscoll, *Active Management of Labour*, pp. 29, 26.
Page 124       Jo Murphy Lawless, *Reading Birth and Death*, p. 24.
Page 125       *Ibid*, pp. 62, 8.
Pages 128-9    O'Driscoll, *op. cit.*, p. 37.
Page 131       Gabrielle Palmer, *The Politics of Breastfeeding*, p. 41.
Page 134       Hrdy, *op. cit.*, 154.
Pages 134-5    *Ibid.*, p. 139.
Page 135       O'Connor, *op. cit.*, p. 105.
Page 135       Clear, *op. cit.*, p. 131.

Page 136    HSE, *National Infant Feeding Survey, p.* 16.
Page 138    Palmer, *op. cit.*, pp. 9, 273.
Page 138    HSE, *op. cit.,* p. 144.
Page 145    *Ibid.* p. 118.
Page 147    Palmer, *op. cit.* p. 228.
Page 147    HSE, *op. cit.,* pp. 73, 42.
Page 148    Palmer, *op. cit.* p. vi.
Page 148    HSE, *op. cit.,* p. 154.
Page 149    Food Safety Authority of Ireland, *FSAI News.* April-May 2007,
            p. 8.
Page 169    Crittenden, *op. cit.*, p. 7.
Page 178    Leach, *op. cit.,* p. 50.
Page 181    Marilyn Waring, *If Women Counted: a New Feminist
            Economics*, pp. 25, 29, 74.
Page 182    Finola Kennedy, *Cottage to Crèche*, p. 73.
Page 183    Jonathon Porritt, *Capitalism: As If the World Matters.* p. 253.
Page 184    Porritt, *op. ci*t., p. 268.

# BIBLIOGRAPHY

Becker, Gary. *A Treatise on the Family*. Cambridge, Massachusetts: Harvard University Press, 1981.

Callan, Tim et al (eds.). *How Unequal? Men and Women in the Irish Labour Market*. Dublin: Economic and Social Research Institute, 2000.

Clear, Caitriona. *Women of the House: Women's Household Work in Ireland 1922-61*. Dublin: Irish Academic Press, 2000.

Corcoran, Mary P. *Irish Illegals: Transients between Two Societies*. Westport, Connecticut, Greenwood Press, 1993.

Crittenden, Ann. *The Price of Motherhood: Why the Most Important Job in the World is Still the Least Valued*. New York: Henry Holt and Company, 2001.

de Marneffe, Daphne. *Maternal Desire: on Children, Love and the Inner Life*. London: Little, Brown, 2004.

Enright, Anne. *The Gathering*. London: Vintage, 2008.

Fennell, Nuala et al. *Can You Stay Married?* Cork and Dublin: Mercier Press, 1972.

Fennell, Nuala. *Irish Marriage: How Are You?* Cork and Dublin: Mercier Press, 1974.

Fennell, Nuala. *Political Woman*. Dublin: Currach Press, 2009.

Ferriter, Diarmuid. *Occasions of Sin: Sex and Society in Modern Ireland*. London: Profile Books, 2009.

Finnegan, Frances. *Do Penance or Perish: Magdalen Asylums in Ireland*. Oxford: Oxford University Press, 2004.

Friedan, Betty. *The Feminine Mystique*. New York: W. W. Norton, 1963.

Friedan, Betty. *The Second Stage*. Cambridge, Massachusetts: Harvard University Press, 1981.

Gerhardt, Sue. *Why Love Matters: How Affection Shapes a Baby's Brain*. London: Routledge, 2004.

Gillespie, Elgy. *Changing the Times – Irish Women Journalists. 1969-81.* Dublin: Lilliput Press, 2003.

Greer, Germaine. *The Female Eunuch*. London: Paladin, 1970.

Hakim, Catherine. *Key Issues in Women's Work: Female Diversity and the Polarisation of Women's Employment*. London: Glasshouse Press 2004.

Heywood, Colin. A History of Childhood. Oxford/Cambridge: Polity Press, 2001.

Hrdy, Sarah Blaffer. *Mother Nature: Maternal Instincts and How They Shape the Human Species*. New York: Ballantine Books, 2000.

Kennedy, Finola. *Cottage to Crèche: Family Change in Ireland.* Dublin: Institute of Public Administration, 2001.

Kenny, Mary. *Woman x Two: How to Cope with a Double Life.* London: Sidgwick and Jackson, 1978.

Kenny, Mary. *Goodbye to Catholic Ireland: a Social, Personal and Cultural History from the Fall of Parnell to the Realm of Mary Robinson.* London: Sinclair-Stevenson, 1997.

Leach, Penelope. *Children First: What Society Must Do –and Is Not Doing – For Children.* Harmondsworth: Penguin, 1994.

Leach, Penelope. *Your Baby and Child.* London: Dorling Kindersley, 2010.

Murphy-Lawless, Jo. *Reading Birth and Death: a History of Obstetric Thinking.* Cork: Cork University Press, 1998.

Ní Dhonnchadha, Máirín el al (eds.). The *Field Day Anthology of Women's Writing.* Cork: Cork University Press, 2002.

O'Brien, John. *The Vanishing Irish.* Benedictine Press, 1952.

O'Connor, Sheila. *Without Consent.* Dublin: Poolbeg, 2010.

O'Driscoll, Kieran et al. *Active Management of Labour.* St Louis, Missouri: Mosby, 2003.

O'Faolain, Nuala. *Are You Somebody?* Dublin: New Island Books, 2007.

O'Faolain, Nuala. *Almost There: The Onward Journey of a Dublin Woman.* New York: Riverhead Books, 2003.

Levine, June. *Sisters.* Swords, County Dublin: Ward River Press, 1982.

Palmer, Gabrielle. *The Politics of Breastfeeding: When Breasts Are Bad for Business.* London: Pinter and Martin, 2009.

Porritt, Jonathon. *Capitalism: As If the World Matters.* London: Earthscan, 2005.

Robins, Joseph. *A Study of Charity Children in Ireland 1700-1900.* Dublin: Institute of Public Administration, 1980.

Ruddock, Norman. *The Rambling Rector.* Dublin: Columba Press, 2004.

Tammet, David. *Born on a Blue Day, Inside the Extraordinary Mind of an Autistic Savant.* New York: Barnes and Noble, 2007.

Waring, Marilyn. *If Women Counted: a New Feminist Economics.* New York: Harper Collins, 1988.

## Conferences, Official and Government Papers and Reports

Cuidiú/Irish Childbirth Trust (www.cuidiu-ict.ie). *Consumer Guide to the Maternity Services in Ireland.*

Department of the Environment, Heritage and Local Government. *Planning Guidelines.* Dublin: June, 2001.

European Commission, *Report on Equality between Women and Men*, 2005.

*Families, Children and Childcare Study.* (www.familieschildrenchildcare. org). London: Institute for the Study of Children, Families and Social Issues, Birkbeck College: 2001–.

Fitzgerald, Eithne. *Cherishing our Children*. Labour Party Policy Proposal on Childcare. Dublin, 2002.

Food Safety Authority of Ireland, *FSAI News,* April-May 2007.

Government Publications. *Report of the First Commission on the Status of Women*. Dublin, 1971.

Government Publications. *Report of the Second Commission on the Status of Women*. Dublin, 1993.

Government Publications. *Strengthening Families for Life: Final Report of the Commission on the Family*. Dublin, 1998.

Government Publications. *The National Children's Strategy*. Dublin, 1999.

Government Publications. *The National Children's Strategy*. Dublin, 2000.

Harding Clarke, Judge Maureen. *Report of the Our Lady of Lourdes Hospital Enquiry*. Dublin, 2006.

Harvard Business Review. *The Required Reading for Executive Women – and the Companies Who Need Them*. 2005.

HSE. *National Infant Feeding Survey*. Dublin, 2008

*Irish Times, The*. 'Sisters: Forty Years of Change in the Lives of Women', 26 May 2010.

KPMG. *Independent Review of Maternity and Gynaecology Services in the Greater Dublin Area,* 2008.

National Economic and Social Forum. *Early Childhood and Education. Dublin,* 2005.

National Institute of Child Health and Development (US) *Study of Early Childcare and Youth Development*. Bethesda, Maryland, 1991–.

National Women's Council of Ireland. *An Accessible Childcare Model*. Dublin, 2005.

National Women's Council of Ireland. *Pensions: What Women Want*. Dublin, 2008.

OECD. *Babies and Bosses: Reconciling Work and Family Life: Ireland, Austria and Japan*. 2003.

Rogan,W.J. 'Cancer from PCBs in Breastmilk? A Risk Benefit Analysis'. North Carolina: US National Institute of Environmental Health Sciences, 1989.

UN Convention on the Rights of the Child, 1989.

UNICEF. *Innocenti Declaration on the Protection, Promotion and Support of Breastfeeding*. 1990.

Walsh, Thomas. 'A Historical Overview of our Conceptualisation of Childhood in Ireland in the 20th Century', presented at the conference *Voices and Images of Childhood and Adolescence: Rethinking Children's Lives*. Dublin, 2004.

WHO/UNICEF. *Ten Steps to Successful Breastfeeding*, 1998.